words
music
and
the
church

words music and the church

Erik Routley

nashville   ABINGDON PRESS   new york

WORDS, MUSIC, AND THE CHURCH

Copyright © 1968 by Abingdon Press

Library of Congress Catalog Card Number: 68-11479

Scripture quotations unless otherwise noted are
from the Revised Standard Version of the Bible,
copyrighted 1946 and 1952 by the Division of
Christian Education, National Council of Churches,
and are used by permission.
Scripture quotations noted NEB are from the
New English Bible, New Testament. © the Dele-
gates of the Oxford University Press and the Syndics
of the Cambridge University Press 1961. Reprinted
by permission.

SET UP, PRINTED, AND BOUND BY THE
PARTHENON PRESS, AT NASHVILLE,
TENNESSEE, UNITED STATES OF AMERICA

dedicated
with respect and gratitude
to
Lloyd A. Pfautsch

preface

When President McCord of Princeton Theological Seminary invited me (in December of 1962) to deliver the 1966 Stone Lectures, he suggested that they should deal with contemporary church music. At the time I was working on the final draft of a book which has since been published under the title of *Twentieth Century Church Music*. I wondered whether by 1966 there would be enough to add to that book to make it safe to accept President McCord's honorific invitation. But I said at the time that so much was happening that it would indeed be safe. I thought I should be able to lecture on contemporary church music without repeating myself.

I could have done so—that is to say, the subject is indeed expanding so quickly that "Church Music, 1962–1966" would have provided ample material for a course of five lectures. But that is not how it has turned out. It seemed to me, during the intervening time, that it would be better if I could make some attempt to deal theologically with the subject that my previous book treats annalistically. That would mean mentioning some of the subjects that the other book handles, but approaching them from a different direction.

But candor compels me to admit that this was not all. When the other book was commissioned, I had been less than two years in the ministry of an ordinary Congregational church in Scotland. At the date of writing this, I had completed seven years in that work. I was simply unable to resist the conviction that, if I could, I must try to speak rather more pastorally, less academically, than I originally intended to do.

What I offer here, then, is a discourse which I hope will be of equal interest to people who are concerned with music and to people who are seriously involved in the ongoing work of the church in this perilous and inspiriting age. I write not only against the background of developments in music, but against that of the new dissent from orthodox theology. I write (I cannot help it, situated as I am) in the age in which everybody has heard of Bonhoeffer and the Bishop of Woolwich. I write as one who personally believes Harvey Cox's *Secular City* to be one of the great books of our time. I wrote, precisely, from a traditionally religious city that is just learning to be secular—Edinburgh. Nobody who carries on an ordinary ministry can be unaware of how preposterous and incomprehensible the things he loves most look to anybody in the secular world who notices them at all. No such person interested in church music can ignore the fact that church music seems peculiar, if not downright corrupt, to a secular musician. One of the things that I have come to regard as ridiculous is the academic criticism of popular church music like hymns, which was fashionable ten or twenty years ago, and which some still believe in.

If somebody from the secular world comes and asks me what we think we are doing when we play and sing in church, I want to have an answer. I believe that others do also; therefore, I have the temerity thus to publish my provisional findings. I am committed to the spirit of inquiry which prompts much contemporary theological revolt, but not to its spirit of pessimism and only very marginally to its spirit of apology or iconoclasm. My assumption is that these are tremendous days, but not that they are hopeless days. There is one very large roadblock which I want to see removed, but my conviction is that the power that makes progress possible once it has gone is still there.

I thank the authorities at Princeton for providing the opportunity for pursuing this uncomfortable and risky project. I accept responsibility for its defects. I dare to hope that it will prompt better things from somebody else.

ERIK ROUTLEY
Newcastle-upon-Tyne
December, 1967

contents

I
vanishing
orthodoxies

1. the old men

A Formula from Tillich

Paul Tillich (it is still difficult to think of the world without him!) in one of his earlier and less publicized works, *Biblical Religion and the Search for Ultimate Reality*, wrote a paragraph which gives us a useful formula:

Faith, in the biblical view, is an act of the whole personality. Will, knowledge, and emotion participate in it. It is an act of self-surrender, of obedience, of assent. Each of these elements must be present. Emotional surrender without assent and obedience would by-pass the personal center. It would be a compulsion and not a decision. Intellectual assent without emotional participation distorts religious existence into a nonpersonal, cognitive act. Obedience of the will without assent and emotion leads into a depersonalizing slavery. Faith unites and transcends the special functions of the human mind; it is the most personal act of the person. But each function of the human mind is inclined to a kind of imperialism. It tries to become independent and to control the others. Even biblical religion is not without symptoms of these trends. Faith sometimes approaches the point of emotional ecstasy, sometimes the point of mere moral obedience, sometimes the point of cognitive subjection to an authority.[1]

If we extract from that paragraph the formula: Emotion, Knowledge, Will, we have there a trinity of forces which operate in a complete personality, and which therefore we may expect to be operating—or to be operating in distortion—in any considerable personal activity and in the history of cultures. It is my purpose here to apply it to music, and in this field we shall find it especially useful because there is one property which is common to the operation of music and to that history with which, at national or cosmic level, the Bible is concerned. The property is that both are intimately bound up with *time*. Faith is the center of the biblical system precisely because it is the nexus between man, who lives in time, and God, who is the creator of time and therefore timeless. Faith, says Tillich so felicitously, is a harmony of three movements in the human spirit. This means that faith is a property of the whole of life, not something technically, still less denominationally, religious. His analysis of the personal faith of a religious man will help us if we can see an architectural repetition of the same analytic pattern in history, and in that part of history which is music-making. Without attempting either a detailed analysis of the history of music or indeed going over more than a period of a hundred years or the manifestations of one single culture, we can show how handy Tillich's analysis is for the understanding of the present position of church music. We can refer to three historic periods in music and culture, all discernible during the past hundred years and definable not by date

---

[1] (Chicago: University of Chicago Press, 1955), p. 53.

so much as by prevailing attitudes and tendencies. Very broadly they correspond to periods, or attitudes, called romantic, neo-orthodox, and modern.

Three Twentieth-Century Church Pieces

Let us then take first three pieces of church music, all written for the same resources and all written to be performed within the accepted liturgy of any major denomination. They are the "Magnificat in G," by Charles Villiers Stanford, the anthem "Lord, thou hast been our refuge," by Ralph Vaughan Williams, and the anthem, "Sing we merrily," by Frederick Rimmer (Figs. 1-3).[2]

A short description of these three works will be enough to introduce them and to indicate their historic value.

Stanford's Magnificat in G (Fig. 1) is part of his *Full Service in G*, composed in 1904, and that *Full Service* is itself one of five famous settings of the Prayer Book Canticles by this composer which together form a small corpus of church music of the greatest historic significance. As a group of compositions they represent the contribution made by Stanford to the rescuing of church music from Victorian triviality, and if there were no others from his pen (in fact there are many) they would by themselves represent a major achievement in English church music. The five services were written over the period 1879–1909, the first (in B flat) being his opus 10, the last (in C) being opus 115. The G major service is opus 81.

This setting of the Magnificat is a tour de force in that it calls for a highly accomplished boy soprano solo throughout its course; the solo voice sings with, or in antiphony

---

[2] "Magnificat in G" published by Novello, recorded on Argo RG 99; "Lord, thou hast been our refuge" published by Curwen, recorded on Argo RG 340; "Sing we merrily" published by Novello, recorded on D'Art 12-4.

Fig. 1

Magnificat

C. V. STANFORD

God my Sav - ior. _____

pp legato
For he hath re - gard - ed the

pp legato
For he hath re - gard - ed the

pp legato
For he hath re - gard. - ed the

8' only

f
For be - hold _____ from _____

low - li - ness of his hand - maid - en,

low - li - ness of his _____ hand - maid - en,

low - li - ness of his _____ hand - maid - en,

21

Fig. 2

Lord, Thou Hast Been Our Refuge

Motet for Chorus, Semi-Chorus and Orchestra (or Organ)

R. VAUGHAN WILLIAMS

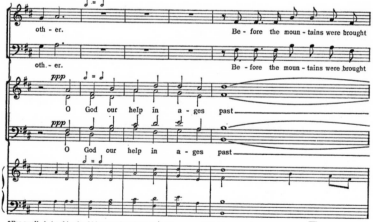

Fig. 3

Sing We Merrily

Anthem for SATB and Organ

PSALM 81, vss 1-4

FREDERICK RIMMER

with, the full choir, and the accompaniment is decorated with an almost unbroken flowing figure in eighth-notes. The picture in the composer's mind is thus described by E. H. Fellowes: "In writing this, Stanford had the idea in his mind that, in accordance with Jewish custom at the period, the Blessed Virgin might have been little more than a child at the time of the birth of Christ; so he pictured her with a spinning-wheel happily singing *Magnificat*." [3]

The modern composers of Stanford's youth were Wagner and Brahms, and (unlike most continental musicians) Stanford had a profound admiration for both. This piece, like most of his church music, shows a very secure sense of musical form, deals in long phrases, and has all the poise of a classic. By anybody's standards it makes a most delectable sound. It is written, in fact, in the idiom of the time: it is, by the standards of 1904, contemporary church music. There is no hint in it of the revolutionary movements in music that are at the time just beginning. Moreover, it is innocently pictorial. There is no hint of the ferocity of the Magnificat (in its Old Testament associations), and even the strong tradition of dignity and majesty in church music of the time, which Stanford follows in his later service in C, gives way to the charming, though certainly not necessarily authentic, idea of the child-wife of Joseph rejoicing over the coming birth of her son.

With Vaughan Williams' profound and celebrated anthem "Lord, thou hast been our refuge" (**Fig. 2**), we move into very different country. This setting of the ninetieth psalm is written for double choir and organ, but the organ does not play until the piece is two thirds gone. The date is 1921, when its composer was getting fully into his stride as a composer. Its vocabulary is no longer that of Brahms

[3] E. H. Fellowes, *English Cathedral Music* (London: Methuen, 1941), p. 240.

and the romantics. It is the language of older music. This we see in three distinct ways: first, in the plainsong-like *recitative* in the opening section sung in unison by the first choir; second, in the parallel chords at "As soon as thou scatterest them"—a device which becomes very familiar in this composer's work; and third, in the use of the hymn tune, "O God, our help in ages past" against the opening recitative, and also to provide the subject of the closing *fugato*. The bars are irregular: the rhythm is sensitively assimilated to the rhythm of speech. In this—as in any other church work of Vaughan Williams—we see a totally new musical *ethos*—the principle that music derived from the remote past can revitalize a tired musical vocabulary and diction. This, of course, was the statement that Vaughan Williams consistently made throughout fifty years of abundant composing, and its effect on his younger contemporaries was profound and ineradicable. To the ears of 1921 his anthem sounded strange, but certainly not discordant or esoteric or incomprehensible.

Turn then to Frederick Rimmer's "Sing we merrily" (Fig. 3). Here we have a setting of the opening verses of Psalm 81, published in 1963 and sung at the opening service of the Edinburgh International Festival in 1964. Here is a different world again. Gone are both the vital and seductive melodiousness of the Stanford, and the majestic meditative devotion of the Vaughan Williams. We are now back to "contemporary" music, and in this sense Rimmer is like Stanford. We are in an idiom that reacts violently against the immediate past, and there we find common ground with Vaughan Williams. But Rimmer reacts by thrusting toward the future, by using a certain musical technique which, though it has been known for forty years or so, is still the subject of hot debate. He produces sounds very strange even to contemporary ears, violent dissonances, dramatic contrasts, and dangerous juxtapositions of sound.

In fact, this music is partly written in the "twelve-tone" style, of which it will be enough to say here simply that it is one of the earliest of those modern styles which react decisively against all the traditional romantic and classical notions of inspiration, of beauty, and of musical effect. Of this I shall have more to say at a later stage.[4] It renounces all the traditional devices of grace and winsomeness, such as four-part vocal harmony (of which it has none) and long melodic phrases, for the sake of a steely intellectual integrity. Its effect is startling, but nobody can deny its appropriateness to the prophetic ecstasy of which the words speak.

These three pieces of music, composed within a period of sixty years, represent three musical universes of discourse which seem to have very little in common. If we regard these three musical periods, or complexes of attitude, as broadly corresponding to the hegemonies of Emotion, Knowledge and Will, the relation between them will become clear, and we may be able to make certain judgments about what is happening at present and what may happen in the foreseeable future.

Romanticism

Stanford's "Magnificat" is a very good piece of music in what is called the "romantic" style. Vaughan Williams' "Lord, thou hast been our refuge," is an equally good piece in the "historical" style. Frederick Rimmer's "Sing we merrily" is a piece worthy of comparison with the others, but is in the "revolutionary" style. Those descriptive words

---

[4] Those interested in checking this statement will find the "tone-row" in the opening eighth-note figure in the organ accompaniment, and will be able to trace fragments of it throughout the rest of the piece. At certain points it is transposed.

will have to serve, unsatisfactory though they are; they have
at least this advantage, that they at once sound the over-
tone of "time relation." Music moves in time: a piece of
music spans a period of time, and movements in music
history are distinguished by being related in historical time.
I am here suggesting that we can distinguish our three
musical periods by noting the difference between one and
another in their implied attitude to time, and assumptions
about it. This is better than assigning the three attitudes to
specific periods of history. In the year 1909, for example,
Stanford was writing his "service in C," which is pure
romantic; Vaughan Williams was already writing music
in the historical style; and Debussy and Schönberg had already begun to make an impact on the public consciousness
with revolutionary styles that denied most of the fundamental assumptions of orthodox classical music. People are
still writing music in the romantic style, or in a post-
Vaughan Williams historical style. Chopping history up
into "periods" has little relevance to aesthetic history. But
if one looks at the internal attitudes to time to be found in
these three schools or cultures of music-making, what
emerges at once is a clear division between them in the
emphases which they place on the present, the past, and
the future.

Much has been said about romanticism, and I wish to
dispute none of it. It seems profitable here simply to attend to the fact that the romantic culture in art is present-
centered; this is not far from saying that it is the culture
in which emotional response is paramount. It is in the
handling of emotion, in the evoking of immediate affective
response, that the romantics excel. Other things are sub-
ordinated to this primary aim.

Romantic writers, philosophers, and artists devote their
positive attention and statements to the present; the past

and the future are illustrative—they are not objects of study in their own right. A glance at the use that Romantics make of the past confirms this. Consider how Sir Walter Scott used history in his novels—it was nothing to him that his history was not precise. What he aimed to do was to exalt the *present* glory and grace of a Scotland that had lost its nerve and its national integrity, by referring constantly to its past. The past illustrated and confirmed what he wanted to say about the present. Or consider the cult of the past that we find in Tennyson's Arthurian idylls, or Kingsley's retelling of Greek myths: a legendary or mythological past suits the romantic purpose as well as—perhaps better than—a verifiable historical past (because you have license to make what you can of legend and myth). Above all, consider William Blake, in whom you can contrast his hatred of classical culture with his use of strange esoteric mythology: Blake's famous lines beginning "And did those feet in ancient time . . ." are pure romanticism in that, while they are introduced by a violent attack on all forms of scholarly classical historic culture, they themselves express a powerful present resolution ("I will not cease from mental fight . . ."), backed by a vivid and unverifiable legend (that Jesus in his infancy may have stayed in Somerset).

The success-culture of the Victorian Age produced a form of romantic culture in society—an emotional response to achievement, to the large-scale successful man, to the present conquest of nature by man's invention. European culture in the nineteenth century, and British culture above all, emphasized the present; "All the past we leave behind," sang Whittier in America. Protest against present evils and sufferings brought about by the Industrial Revolution was produced by the Revolution itself. Cornish peasants in John Wesley's time were not protesting about

their poverty, and when John Wesley voiced the protest
for them it was largely in terms of their deprivation of
gospel promises for the spiritual future rather than in terms
of their deprivation of the rights of citizens in this world.
Wesley left his lay disciples to begin on that more present
protest, and even so, the most violent and present-centered
protests in social affairs came from freethinkers, disciples of
the French Revolution like Tom Paine. In philosophy,
what could be more present-centered than John Stuart
Mill's utilitarianism? In economics, what could be more
so than the characteristic comment of the Forsytes in
Galsworthy's saga, looking at a great picture: "What will
it fetch?"

In church affairs the most decisive revolution of the
British nineteenth century was the Oxford Movement in
the Church of England. That was partly a revival of historical sense—a returning to the pre-Reformation innocence
of the Middle Ages, a bringing back of old ritual, a return
to the ascetic priestly holiness of the saints. But again, history was being used for a present revolutionary purpose.
The new cult of history inspired in the church by Newman,
Keble, and Pusey led directly to what we are about to dis-
cuss in the next period. But what it in fact was associated
with in the first generation of the Oxford Movement was a
direct ministry to the new industrial poor. Christian social-
ism was inseparable from the new movement. The history
it was based on was imprecise enough: no modern critical
historian would for a moment accept the idea of medieval
innocence and grandeur that the Tractarians canvassed so
strenuously. The effect was present-centered—the revival of
the Church of England and the helping of the new poor.
To this day in England you are likely to find the most advanced "Catholic" practices in an ugly Victorian building
near the railway station, rather than in a country parish

church of medieval magnificence, or indeed in a vintage
1905 suburban church.

Romanticism suddenly extends the range of emotional
evocation and response by introducing *remoteness* into
everything. Hence, on the one hand, there is the love of
legend and myth; on the other, the association of exalted
poetry with the contemplation of natural objects and every-
day experiences (as in Wordsworth). Hence also, we may
say, the typically Romantic attitude toward the future.

The romantic is an optimist in regard to the future. It is,
to him, the place of dreams and visions. Addington
Symonds' poem including the lines "These things shall be"
is a typical uncritical vision of the future. So is Tennyson's
"Locksley Hall." American hymns of the time are full of
references to the future:

> For lo! the days are hastening on,
>   By prophet-bards foretold,
> When with the ever-circling years,
>   Comes round the age of gold. (Sears)

> And lo! already on the hills
>   The flags of dawn appear;
> Gird up your loins, ye prophet souls,
>   Proclaim the day is near. (Hosmer)

The future is an object of confidence—it will see the
vindication of human nature, and above all, the eradication
of the *present* evils of war, poverty, and unbelief. All those
things which in the nineteenth century seemed to give
ground for optimism have in the twentieth century shown
us their undersides: the bomb, the population explosion,
brainwashing, and pornography are not the bastards but the
legitimate children of scientific research, medicine, psychology and literacy—all born of the romantic age.

Romantic Music

Therefore, the romantic age is the age of sensuously beautiful music—and, of course, of its perversions. Stanford's "Magnificat" is the work of a man who aims chiefly at capturing beauty. It is romantic in its naïve pictorial approach to its subject, in its deployment of large musical resources, and in its immediate evocation of emotion. It is not historical music—its style is that of the composers immediately preceding its own composer. It makes no attempt to ask questions or to voice doubts about beauty or form or melody, the qualities that have been assumed in music for three hundred years and specifically sought by composers for at least a century.

Of all romantic composers in the grand style, my own choice is unquestionably Schubert. Here is the composer without any patron to give him a living, writing music as it comes to him, conditioned much less than Beethoven— enormously less than Haydn—by the demands and support of people who would pay for his music. He protested not decisively or specifically as Mozart did against patronage, but naïvely, through his personality and habits against the world's standards of system and success; he wrote music strictly "in the present," on odd bits of paper when it came to him, without any thought of its being preserved for an admiring or industrious posterity, without much consideration for the music of other composers before him. His music evokes the most profound and poignant crises of response in the listener—his sense of tragedy is as catastrophic as anybody's, not excluding Beethoven (for surely it is not strictly in his handling of *tragedy* that Beethoven is at his most sublime). He provides pure beauty wherever he puts pen to paper—exquisite pleasure, whether in serenity or in the contemplation of such mysteries of remoteness as one encounters in the G major String Quartet, is his

simple and achieved aim. Schubert is directly behind
Brahms, and Brahms behind Stanford; and when any of
them or their contemporaries wrote music, they wrote it as
free men who dared—in the confidence of their unques-
tioned skill and of a field of reference which was settled and
not subject to doubt—to explore all the mysteries of life.
So you get, in this sense, the possibilities of "great art"—
large public gestures that move multitudes, grand-scale
portrayals of human situations in language essentially stately
and intelligible. It is not really subjectivism that is the mark
of the great romantic; it is confidence in the present, an
imperial attitude toward the past and the future which
annex them for the benefit of the present. The subjective,
the trivial, the boring, the overornate, the ill-proportioned
are natural perversions of romantic art. Romanticism spread
an infectious confidence which in too many artists extinguished self-criticism; its associated culture put so much
wealth into circulation that too many bad artists, composers, and architects had too little economic worry to curb
their exuberance. But at their best (and what a galaxy there
was, even in the one field of music!) the romantics were,
in the strict sense, magnificent.

Pedagogy

The next phrase grew naturally out of romanticism. I
would call it the phase of knowledge. Around the turn of
the century we hear a new kind of voice speaking. It was
the age when men began to demonstrate the falsity of
Scott's history by finding out the real facts about history;
when people began seriously to inquire whether there was
such a person as King Arthur, and if so, what were his dates;
when men began to apply objective criticism to the Scriptures. Accuracy was all. The messages sent into the human
consciousness by emotion came under scrutiny, and within

this age or phase we find both a return to dogma in the classical sense and a thirst for objective historical precision.[5] In theology we pass through a phase in which everything subjective and emotional is suspected, and only the dogmatic and the scholarly are regarded as worthy of serious attention. It is the age of the great commentaries, the great systematic theologies, the revival of patristic learning, the cult of the "primary source." We notice also a revival of authority, a cooling off of the cult of the self-made hero (whether businessman or preacher), a large number of conversions to Roman Catholicism on the part of intellectuals for whom romance had faded.

Thus, with knowledge, comes pedagogy, and with pedagogy, moralism. Look at all the historical companions to hymnals that the twentieth century has produced, all the dates and qualifications that now go with ascriptions of words and tunes in hymnals, all the cult of original versions and pure texts. And look at all the talk there has been about the difference between good music and bad, all the efforts to "raise standards." More broadly, look at the lust for information, the increasing value put on education, the movements toward adult education, the multiplication of universities: wherever one looks nowadays one sees the end products of the prodigious pedagogic revolution which has its roots in the late Victorian Age and its first fruits in the years just preceding and following the First World War.[6]

---

[5] It was about a hundred years ago (1866) that the now well-known hymn, "The church's one foundation," first appeared. It was a heartfelt protest by a young anglican priest against the sorrow created in the church by the trial of Bishop Colenso in Africa for publishing critical speculations about the Pentateuch.

[6] See Daniel Jenkins, The Educated Society (London: Faber & Faber, 1967).

Pedagogic Music

In music this brought a radical revolution. The fashion of respecting only contemporary music, which had really been the habit among secular musicians ever since the dawn of polyphony [7] had continued well into the nineteenth century. But toward the end of that century we find in many European countries a new interest in national folk music (Kodály in Hungary, Lindeman in Norway, Vaughan Williams in Britain), which brought about a shift of musical emphasis from the accepted centers of Italian and Teutonic culture to the countries which in, say, 1825, were hardly thought of as musical at all. Parallel to this there was a new cult of musical scholarship—the revival of plainsong, the correction of earlier approximations to old music, and above all the new interest in the music of the European sixteenth century.

Vaughan Williams in England was a typical product of this movement—indeed, he was its first popularizer in England. The two parallel cults of Pre-Raphaelite primitivism and of scholarship changed the language of music, especially of church music, and changed the habits of the music lover almost beyond recognition.

Look, for example, at the resurrection of the music of J. S. Bach—the first major development in historical music making. Bach was a forgotten composer for the best part of eighty years after his death. Mendelssohn and the two musical Wesleys pioneered the movement to bring his music back to public performance. It was hardly otherwise with Schubert, so much of whose work had to be unearthed

---

[7] See F. Goldbeck, "Twentieth Century Composers and Tradition" in R. H. Myers' (ed.) *Twentieth Century Music* (London: John Calder Publishers, 1960), and a comment on this in my own *Twentieth Century Church Music* (New York: Oxford University Press, 1964), pp. 113-16.

and published posthumously. Those were early examples. But now, several generations later, there is a massive academic tradition which is systematically bringing the work of forgotten composers back to public life (or bringing it to public life for the first time); the revival of the Tudor and pre-Tudor English composers has its parallel in the steady stream of forgotten eighteenth-century works by composers like Telemann and Steinmetz and the less eminent Bachs which is enriching the concert and stereo repertory.

A handy example of the two phases in the familiar area of church music is in the tunes "Veni Creator Spiritus" (**Fig. 4**) and "Pange Lingua" (**Fig. 5**) which exist nowadays in two parallel versions, often both to be found in the same hymnal.

Fig. 4   Veni Creator

Fig. 5   Pange Lingua

There is a version of both tunes known as the "Mechlin" version (from the abbey in the place now known as Malines) which was made in 1848. Here the old plainsong tune has been revived, but adapted to sound like a tune written about 1800. Its rhythm and accentuation are altered to conform with this demand. The other version in both cases is based on the scholarship of Solesmes, which flourished a generation later, and reproduces the tune exactly as it appears in the manuscripts. There precisely we have the two ways of using the past. The first version is like Walter Scott's history—history adapted to nineteenth-century habits. The second is historian's history—history speaking for itself in its own tongue.

This primitivism is the mark of the phase of knowledge. You have no business, say its exponents, to be ignorant of the past; but neither should you see the past only in terms of your own age. So Vaughan Williams in his anthem here cited not only writes in the style of plainsong and of musical *organum* (tenth-century harmony in parallel fifths), but incorporates into his anthem a two-hundred-year-old hymn tune. You can see the distinctiveness of the "knowledge" technique if you compare Vaughan Williams' plainsong with either the mock plianson in Liszt's *Via Crucis* or the impressionistic monastic noises in Debussy's *La Cathédrale Engloutie* or Ketelby's *In a Monastery Garden*. You further see Vaughan Williams' scholarly primitivism if you study the cadences in any piece of his music you care to take up. They are always based on modal harmony; scarcely ever are they the plain "perfect cadence" that presupposes the musical language of Bach-to-Brahms orthodoxy.

Modern church music owes most of its vitality to this cult of knowledge, and to the pedagogy that went with it, which made Vaughan Williams himself say in his preface to the *English Hymnal* (1906) that good taste is a moral concern. Knowledge sought to discipline emotion. But there was a fatal weakness here. The exclusive cultivation of knowledge, with its past-centered habits, can lead to a kind of death wish, a failure to come to terms with the present, a negligence about the future, which there has been time for us to notice in our own recent past.

2. the new men

A Formula from C. P. Snow

When Sir Charles Snow (then known as C. P. Snow) gave the celebrated lecture called *The Two Cultures and Scientific Revolution*[1] he exposed a certain corruption which I suggest lies at the heart of the cult of Knowledge. Near the beginning of that lecture he uncovered a truth about the age in which he had been brought up (which corresponds pretty well with our phase of Knowledge) which so scandalized his hearers, and later his readers, that most of us spent a frenzied month or two trying to find reasons why he could not be right. Then we gave up and decided that he must be. I myself am not sure that his case could not have been better stated in another way, but this is what he said. He said it about what he called the "first culture" (that of letters and humanities, as distinguished from that of science); but I think he was saying it about past-centered Knowledge.

I remember being crossexamined by a scientist of distinction. "Why do most writers take on social opinions which would have been thought distinctly uncivilized and démodé at the time

[1] (Cambridge: Cambridge University Press, 1959).

of the Plantagenets? Wasn't that true of most of the famous twentieth-century writers? Yeats, Pound, Wyndham Lewis, nine out of ten of those who have dominated literary sensibility in our time—weren't they not only politically silly, but politically wicked? Didn't the influence of all that they represent bring Auschwitz that much nearer? [2]

If you have been following me, you may object that he was talking not about Knowledge but about romanticism. No: this was the age in which men had no illusions about the past (scholarship was dispersing them), and in which nineteenth-century successes were turning sour.

> This is the way the world ends
> Not with a bang but a whimper.[3]

Eliot's symbolic lines come from the very age which gave the word "academic" a bad name—the name of remote and detached unconcern. Elevate a concern for the particularities of the past into a sovereign principle, and what you get is the deathwish, whether it be expressed in an affectation of loneliness and pessimism or in Auschwitz. ("Intellectual assent without emotional participation distorts . . . existence into a nonpersonal cognitive act," said Tillich.) Where the romantic age turned Arthur's knights into contemporary gentlemen, and "Veni Creator" into a pleasantly rounded popular tune, by these means at least making some kind of contemporary use of the past, the age of knowledge could, through its preoccupation with the past, degenerate into a contempt of the present and an acceptance of an imponderable and terrifying future through total neglect of one's responsibilities for it. It became nonpersonally

[2] *Ibid.*, p. 7.
[3] From "The Hollow Men" in T. S. Eliot's *Collected Poems, 1909-1962* (New York: Harcourt, Brace & World, 1963). Used by permission of Harcourt, Brace & World and Faber & Faber.

cognitive: it produced, at its worst, unpreachable scholarship, anti-existential dogma, and the flight from true personal encounter even with the truth.

But recall that it did produce Vaughan Williams, whose music, whatever else it is, is not nonpersonal or passionless. But it is the worst in an age against which good men in the next age react, and this situation is that out of which what we now call modern music grew. I want first to establish that the asperities of modern music have a perfectly intelligible cause; if we can believe this we may also believe that it has an intelligible and hopeful future. If the church is going to make any sense out of all this, it will have to move fairly quickly in order to recover the ground it has chosen to lose. That is another story to which I shall refer later.

Modern Music's Cultural Background

I must not be tempted to treat as history an age through which we are at present passing; but it is hardly controversial to point out that this is an age of restlessness, and to hazard the guess that it is by the same token an age of great creativeness. In particular it is in violent reaction against Knowledge and pedagogy. The past in any given field is now treated with indulgence, even with a sort of remote respect, but quite without the veneration it enjoyed recently. Authority is not only challenged everywhere, it is not now a source of pleasurable repose. (The detective story is giving ground to science fiction or the spy thriller; the friendly policeman is in danger of losing most of his hold on the literate imagination.) The idea that priority must be given to what is past, or to what is *given* (in the philosophical sense) has yielded place to the idea that what matters now is the future. It would be too facile to say this if we meant "future" in the merely historical sense. It is more precise and more reliable to argue that this is the age, in Tillich's sense, of the Will.

In theology this is easily checked. There is hardly any major field of church life in which the tide is not running away from tradition, away from academic detachment, and toward personal involvement with the world. Tillich himself has made historic assaults on what I am here defining as the culture of knowledge. In a very different way, *Honest to God* represents, very faithfully, "will" over against both knowledge and emotion in its resolute questioning of the position of the orthodox of the twentieth century. The history of the Roman Catholic Church during the past 150 years reflects the movement from emotional romanticism via scholarship toward involvement. Vernacular liturgy, to take the most obvious example, is a gesture of involvement, defying the respect for the past (and for authority) implied in the universal use of Latin (commonly and with shocking inaccuracy called a "dead" language). Or take our folk attitude to the Scriptures. In 1850 they were venerated innocently; in 1900 they were under scholarly and archaeological criticism; now they exist in a multitude of new translations. The Bible of 1850 was held to be beautiful and authoritative; that of 1900 was an object of academic skepticism; that of 1960 is a communicator to the present and immediately future age.[4]

---

[4] The reference to *Honest to God* suggests that quite often this historic process repeats itself in a personal life. *Honest to God* is the composition of John A. T. Robinson, Bishop of Woolwich, who had in his earlier years established himself as a ripe and precise scholar in the New Testament and as a liturgist. Many of his theological associates are similarly scholars. If I may be permitted to compare small things with great, I find that I have written books on my specialist subject in all three modes, without any conscious intention of "making progress." I have written romantically, in endeavoring to make the classic hymnwriters speak to our own age, sometimes (as I now see) preferring what the age would understand to what the authors intended (*I'll Praise My Maker* and *Hymns and the Faith*); I have written historically (*Hymns and Human*

Existential approaches to philosophy are equally anti-romantic and anti-historical. The thrust of Sartre's famous epigram on man's predicament—*jeté là comme ça*—is a thrust to the future. It might seem that the existential view of things is a view anchored to the present; but that is to analyze it incorrectly. The characteristic positivist or existential reaction against dogma is not to say, "I will explore what I feel about this," but rather, "I will see what this, stripped of all prior associations, *does*." Linguistic philosophy examines the properties of words, not for what emotions they arouse, but for what they communicate— what happens when they move in time toward the future. It is neither a dogmatic system nor a private experience to which the linguistic philosopher refers the words he analyzes; it is to the ongoing community of speakers and hearers. Significantly, his popular way of describing a misuse of words (as he judges it) is to say, "that's poetry"—referring the disorder both to the introduction of the conventions of the past and to the unseasonable intervention of private emotion. So, in analyzing, in the contemporary way, the linguistics of the Christian faith, all the pressure is against superstition and self-deception, and toward communication.[5] We have now accepted in common theological currency the blessed word "demythologizing," which magnificently sums up the whole story: suspect the myth; test it against history; retranslate the concept avoiding the myth. That is precisely the process—pass through emotion and knowledge toward will.

Now in music we see the pressure of our time in the

Life); but my last effort was in the direction of examining hymns existentially and relating them to the future (*Hymns Today and Tomorrow*). This seems, now that I have noticed it, to be a perfectly natural process.

[5] See, for example, Paul van Buren, *The Secular Meaning of the Gospel* (New York: Macmillan Paperbacks, 1965) and Donald Evans, *The Logic of Self-Involvement* (Napierville, Ill.: Alec R. Allenson, Inc., 1963).

greatly accelerated speed of experiment which the musicians are permitting themselves. It is because of our present fashion of thinking and responding to the human situation that "modern" music has become what it has become—something astounding, something which in its extreme manifestations causes musical people to attack it as not being music at all.

Music of the "modern," or as we are wont to say, "avant-garde" kind may be music playable on conventional instruments, or music that renounces conventional instruments altogether. It may even be "composed" (if that is the right word) through a computer. Experiments of this kind have been conducted at Princeton. All this music is part of the reaction against musical dogma and convention which goes back to Debussy (1862-1918); and Debussy was essentially a romantic composer. But he fastened on the individualistic, adventurous aspect of romanticism, and conducted in some of his music experiments with sound sensations which provoked a hostile reaction from the neoscholastic musicians of the second phase in Britain and Germany, and kept him on the fringe of the music-lover's accepted repertory during the first forty years of this century. But when Debussy listened to the actual sounds made by bells, and transcribed it for the piano, he proved to be not only the last of the romantic musical naturalists, but the first of the musical scientists.

And that is what matters. What needs to be understood is basically this: first, that the new music is partly a new encounter between music and science; and second, that the special quality of the new music is derived from a new approach to the philosophical questions of choice and probability in the process of composition. Neither of these are new inventions; they are approaches from new directions to matters which have always been at the heart of music making. It is on this ground that the new music, however strange it sounds, must be regarded as music and not as some sort of para-music or imitation music.

Music and the New Science

Music has always been a process of applied physics. There is nothing essentially different in using an electronic sound-producing device for purposes of organized musical composition from using a pipe in which a column of air is caused to vibrate, or a string whose vibrations are controlled by altering the active length. At that elementary level, music which uses conventional instruments in an unconventional way (as when the violinist is directed to activate his strings with the wood of the bow instead of the hair) is not really discontinuous with the old music that uses the same instruments; neither are the newly invented instruments discontinuous with instruments of venerable pedigree. But that is not all of what we mean by the encounter between music and science.

The heart of the matter is reached when we ask what we now mean by science. There has been a subtle change (but by now we shall find it an expected change) in what we mean by that word. To the nonscientist, science perhaps means the discovery of the laws of nature, the building up of a dogmatic system of chemistry, physics, mathematics, or whatever the subject is, and a consequent control of nature. It is still possible—and it is still the disastrous habit of the nonscientists—to take a romantic or a noetic view of science, so that to us, outside his world, the scientist becomes either a worker of marvels or a sinister dogmatist who among other things is bent on destroying religious belief. We ought to know by now that if we either admire the scientist or vilify him on these grounds we are flogging a horse that has been dead many years if it ever was alive.

The scientist proceeds on a dogma that contains one article only—that inquiry is free. We have recently had to thank John Wren-Lewis for making this elementary fact articulate, and for recalling us to the truth with which the scientist really is concerned. He is no moralist, but neither is he an iconoclast. The whole difference between modern (post-Newtonian) science and what passed for science in the days when the Magi visited Bethlehem is the difference between an observer who presupposed a supernatural order into which he fitted his observations, and an observer who simply watches and records his findings. Wren-Lewis' point is, indeed, that had it not been for the gospel brought by Jesus Christ, the gospel which delivered men from the fear of a remote, unapproachable, irrational God into a state of conversation with a rational, approachable, and patient God who showed himself in human flesh, there would have been no modern science at all. It is the gospel which gives men confidence to walk freely among the mysteries of the created world, instead of living in a world where such beliefs as those expressed (and refuted) in Hebrews 12:18-24 (the passage about the mountain which no living creature could touch and remain alive) were common currency.

The scientist then is a free inquirer, asking the question first and seeking only to control the world of nature in accordance with the principles which he discovers. He is in conflict with no religion except that of superstition—that is, the religion that presupposes propositions which are unapproachable by reason, and which permit no question to be asked and no dissent to be attempted. That is the true meaning of a scientific age.

When it comes to music, the encounter between music and science means the musician's new attitude toward conventional musical dogma. It means a freedom which sometimes moves an unsophisticated listener to comment with horror on its license—its use of dissonance, its defiance of the conventions of melody, and its employment of strange sound making devices.

What Stockhausen Said

Let a contemporary leader in avant-garde music illustrate this. Karlheinz Stockhausen recently said (in a lecture given in Cambridge on November 28, 1965, and in other places in Britain) two things which are relevant to this point.

First he explained how in one of his own pieces he experimented with rhythm and space. The rhythmic experiment was based on the extension of what we normally call rhythm to include the patterns made by the vibrations contained in audible sounds. Normally when we say "rhythm" in music, we mean a pattern made in time by successive musical stresses—the triple rhythm of a waltz, the duple rhythm of a march, or the free rhythm of plainsong. The "beats" of these rhythms are normally separated by audible time intervals. But it is possible to say that any audible note is itself a rhythm, because it consists of a series of impulses or vibrations. Whereas the downbeats of "The Blue Danube" come approximately once a second, the impulses in the sound called Middle C come 256 times a second; but since both are a function of impulse, there is a continuity between one kind of pattern and the other. What happens if you try to establish an audible connection between these two rhythms? It cannot be done with a conventional instrument, but it can be done, of course, with an electronic device, and Stockhausen has demonstrated what happens when it is done. Again, he spoke of experiments in the spatial separation of sounds—the use, that is to say, of the phenomenon familiar to us in stereophonic recordings. Again, this is something to which electronics alone can at present provide free access. I forbear to comment on what all this sounds like; I mention it simply to show how a musician is today using the former kind of encounter between music and science. He is making experiments in the control of nature based on the findings of inquiring scientists. He presents these modern technological findings in a manner which he intends to affect his listener as conventional music affects him. Anyhow, he claims, and with justice, that this is music.

But secondly, Stockhausen said this: that in musical experiment of this kind there is no distinction between "sound" and "noise." "Nothing," he said, "is taboo." He is like the Everest climber who answered the question, "Why did you attempt to climb Everest?" by saying, "Because it's there." If it's there it can be investigated and controlled.

A violent emotional response is the normal reaction to a statement like this. Suddenly the whole army of modern artists, of experimental publishers and playwrights, of enemies of the accepted human conventions seems to rise up before us. Is nothing sacred? "No," says the scientist, and says Stockhausen, "if by sacred you mean untouchable, like the holy mountain in the Old Testament, nothing is sacred." None the less for that, a powerful resistance builds up against the musical experimenters, because they look uncommonly like all the other people whom we fear as subverters of all our moral codes. The emotion becomes one of fear and hostility, and we are moved to dismiss Stockhausen because the sounds he makes sound ugly. "How do you know?" is the musician's disconcerting reply.

It is worthwhile to add, by the way, that since music always was the nearest of the arts to physical science, nobody need be worried about the moral implications of musical experiment. Our resistance to modern music tends to be assimilated to the awkward social difficulties we encounter when we are called on to decide whether four-letter words should be publicly printed in novels or spoken in plays. There are no four-letter words in music. None the less, we often think modern music is a bit naughty or subversive, and not at all the kind of thing that puritans ought to have anything to do with. That must be why musical experiments of this sort are frowned on in that last citadel of bourgeois puritanism, Soviet Russia.

But now let me proceed to the philosophical matter.

Music and the New Man

Broadly speaking, there are in currency today not one but three kinds of music. The kind we are most conscious of is music written by a composer and performed for our listening according to his precise directions. The second kind (which I am leaving to a later stage in this argument) is music which largely depends on improvisation for its effect. The third kind is music that is now technically called "totally organized" or "concrete" or "twelve-tone"—these being three of many categories of music of the avant-garde experimental sort.

The difference between the three musical forms is that the center of *choice* shifts as we pass from one to another. The conventional "classical" kind of music—and anything from Palestrina to Britten will really be found in this category—depends for its effect on the precise following of the composer's directions: what he writes, the performer plays. The *inspiration* is entirely his; interpretation is obedience to the composer's mind. "Inspiration" is partly permitted to the performer in jazz and many other kinds of primitive music; in such a case "inspiration" is shared between him and the composer. But the convention in the kind of music one normally hears at "classical" concerts is that the composer's inspiration will be communicated intact to the listener by the performer.

In all such musical compositions the *effects* are calculated by the composer, and it is here that the chief difference between the music of Benjamin Britten (for example) and that of Stockhausen is to be found. The new musicians ask new questions about the composer's right or duty to control "effect." They suggest that all the composer need do is to control *sound;* the matter of interpretation is left not even to the performer but to the listener himself. If a performer still acts as intermediary between the composer and his audience, then he is given a new kind of freedom. He is not now the servant to be directed but the colleague to be trusted. This, for example, is how Pierre Boulez, another celebrated and sincere *avant-garde* composer, puts it:

People will not fail to put us on trial for "dehumanization." We can answer, on the most elementary level, that far from denying or annihilating him, we reopen the creative circuit to the interpreter, who for a number of years has been asked merely to play the text as "objectively" as possible. Why, what we wind up with is actually a glorification of the interpreter! And not at all an interpreter-robot of terrifying precision, but an interpreter who is involved in what he is doing and is free to make his own choices.[6]

The control of sound in the composer's part may of course be exercised simply by feeding sounds into a reproductive instrument (a tape recorder, for example) and reproducing them when required through amplifier and loudspeakers. In such a case the performer is dispensed with. To those who say that this has extruded all possibility of creative action from the field of music, the experimenters

[6] From "Alea," in *Perspectives of New Music*, Fall–Winter, 1964, p. 53.

reply: "Not at all; the hearer is now free to interpret." Ernst Křenek has this impressive peroration at the end of his article on "The Composer's Influences":

If the composer's inclination to depend on precise computation and strict overall control is the tribute for protection exacted by science, his attitude may be interpreted as a desperate surrender of his prerogative as a sovereign creator relying on the powers of imagination—a reduction of its infinite possibilities to the trivia of verifiable fact. But just as modern science seems to approach areas where the hard-and-fast relationships of old are transfigured into referential patterns having unforseen properties, music organized under the influence of such thought-processes moves on to new imaginative potentialities which might not have been visualized without experience of the scientific influence.[7]

Whatever you may think of the music itself, it is clear that we have moved, with these experimental musicians, from the fields of emotion and knowledge into that of will. The process of creation and decision in experimental music of our time is precisely thrust forward from the composer to the performer, and then to the listener—further and further into the future. The philosophic center—the center of choice and probability—has been moved from the place where we have been brought to expect to find it to a place where we have to learn to find it.

[7] *Ibid.*, p. 41.

II
problems of
authority

3. traditions of disobedience

When the experimental musicians of today, in removing the "choice center" in music from the place where we have always assumed that we should find it, are showing in their world the signs of that moral and philosophical upheaval with which in other worlds my readers are no doubt more familiar. The question we now have to examine is: "Is all this atheistic?"

There is a very powerful predisposition among Christians to believe that it cannot be anything else, and an equal and opposite predisposition among agnostic or atheistic existentialists to suspect any attempt on the Christians' part to come to terms with them. In philosophy and ethics, this has already made itself evident. The only reason why there is less open speech about the atheism of contemporary music is because it is at present a subject of much less general discussion. But the emotional reaction of the ordinary Christian against the more remarkable musical experiments is of the same kind as his reaction against manifestations of existentialism in current Christian moral or philosophical discussion: "It's not suitable." Peaceful coexistence is the best that nine tenths of the people who are aware of the debate at all are ready to expect.

Five Refutations of Classical Fundamentalism

I propose first to try to establish the point that church music is not to be found comfortably settled in the first of my musical categories—that of "classical" or conventional concert music. I want to dislodge the almost universal assumption among Protestants that all music worth attending to is like the music heard at professional concerts, or like the music on which those who study music academically are brought up. "Classical" music is music of controlled effect; but there are other kinds of music, and even the church music that is most familiar is partly to be found among the other kinds.

The presuppositions of "classical" music can easily be isolated if we imagine an eight-year-old child learning to play the piano. His teacher seats him at the instrument, and shows him a printed page with five-line staves and conventional signs on and around those staves. The teacher points to one, points to a certain note on the piano, and says, "Now, *that* sign means *this* note. Whenever you see that sign, play this note." The teacher then shows how different signs require the note to be sounded for a short or a long time, and how different placings on the stave determine pitch; then there has to be a lesson in elementary Italian to teach the child that *largo* means slow, *vivace* means lively, and *allegro* means fast. Dots, dashes, slurs, and all the rest of the musical punctuation signs follow in their due course, and what the child learns nowadays is that all these signs are precise stage directions following a fixed pattern of meaning. In time you know that if the child shows aptitude and perseveres with the rudimentary disciplines, he will be able to play Beethoven's *Hammerklavier*.

This is what we assume when we put our children out to be taught music. The orchestras whom we support and the concerts we pay for supply music which supports this belief. If an orchestral conductor permits his orchestra to deviate from the composer's declared intentions, our music critics will note it against him; if a concert pianist plays not the notes written but some other notes, he will get pejorative reviews. Musicians who play professionally are expected, as the least possible demand, to play exactly what the composer has instructed them to play, no matter how difficult it is, and no matter what they might themselves be wanting to play. No professional musician minds this; he is dedicated to the precise duty of interpreting by obedience. Everybody is happy.

But now note the exceptions to this over-simple statement.

1. Interpretation

In a current hi-fi record catalogue, I note that thirty-one different recordings of Beethoven's *Fifth Symphony* are obtainable in Great Britain. That is a simple demonstration of the fact that there is no such thing as a definitive performance of a classical work of music. It is different with all the other arts: the painter paints his picture, and there it is —finished. A sculptor carves his sculpture, a poet writes his poem, an architect builds his cathedral or his garage. But a musician doesn't just write his symphony. It is "finished" only in a limited sense when he draws the final double bar; but in a much more important sense it is never finished, because neither Klemperer nor Solti nor Dorati nor Malcolm Sargent or any of their heirs in music will ever produce the performance of that symphony which is definitive for all time. The day will never come when you need manufacture only one record of Beethoven's Fifth, or when you need never again hire an orchestra to play it.

One way of saying this is to say that in music, however minute and carefully ordered the composer's instructions are, they are never complete. There will always be a difference between Karajan's and Kleiber's performance of Beethoven's Fifth; and what is more, there will be a difference between Karajan's performance on Monday and Karajan's performance on Tuesday. That is why we buy new records, and why we go to concert after concert. We have not finished with Beethoven's Fifth the first time we have heard it through, nor yet the fiftieth time. All music of this kind is music of fully controlled effect, and yet interpretation is never exhausted, nor can it be fully determined by instructions from the composer.

And of course there is the added hazard that you cannot be absolutely sure that the composer *did* say what he meant, or all that he meant. What about Beethoven's metronome marks, which all conductors agree are too fast? By "too fast," they mean that the indications given by those instructions are contradictory to the indications of intention given in other instructions (and in a large majority of instructions) by the same composer. What about the debate as to whether there should be a *rallentando* at the final statement of the first theme in the first movement of Schubert's "Great" C major symphony (or the corresponding debate about the speed of the "chorale" theme on its final appearance in the last movement of Brahms No. 1)? Those who in either place make a *rallentando* argue that the composers meant it but omitted to mark it. What about the famous disputed note that appears in Chopin's C minor Prelude (**Fig. 6**)?

Fig. 6

Here those who support version "A" say that this literally
follows the manuscript text. Those who follow version "B"
say that it is obviously required musically, and that Chopin
simply forgot to contradict the E natural in the earlier part
of the bar.

And anyway, metronomes apart, how fast is *allegro*? How
slow is *andante*? Compare Toscanini's speed for the funeral
march in Beethoven's *Eroica* with anybody else's, and you
see at once how wide is the field of interpretation where
authority is believed to have broken down.

2. Free Ornament and Cadenza

We have only to go one stage behind classical music,
strictly so called, to move away altogether from the world of
the fully controlled musical effect. The music of J. S. Bach
has endless examples of what this means. Consider, for one
example, the whole principle of musical ornamentation,
which in Bach and his contemporaries is such an important
feature of interpretation. The mordent, the trill, the shake,
the turn, and all the decorations used to give emphasis to
important notes in a melody on an instrument (the organ
or the harpsichord) which cannot express emphasis by
gradations of touch, are today matters of exact scholarship.
But in Bach's time they were matters of convention and
interpretation. Small signs over the notes to be ornamented
gave a guide to the player, but it is only in modern editions
that these signs are replaced by precise notation of the required decoration, and even in these the notation is never
exhaustive. Moreover, continuous melodic decoration is
now thought to have been a custom in the playing of certain

kinds of music by Bach. An example shows this clearly.

In the English Suites which Bach wrote for harpsichord (see especially the A minor and G minor suites) the sarabands are stately melodic movements with a persistent and haunting rhythmic pattern. The saraband in these suites appears in two forms; both are clearly the same piece—the harmonic structure is identical, and so is the general lie of the melody. But in the second form the melody is much more elaborate; it is decorated by all kinds of devices, none of which distracts the mind for a moment from the main purpose of the melody.

Fig. 7   From English Suite in G minor

Now each saraband is designed in two unequal parts, each of which is marked to be repeated. It is perfectly legitimate to play the simpler version the first time, and the elaborate version for the "repeat," then go on to the second half and follow the same process. Here Bach has provided an alternative "interpretation" of his main theme. But now observe what develops from this. One of Bach's most famous organ preludes in the *Orgelbüchlein* is a very simple one based on the Lutheran chorale, "Ich ruf' zu dir" ("I call upon Thee"). The opening line of the chorale as congregationally sung was as follows:

Fig. 8   Ich ruf' zu dir

Wittenberg, 1535

The corresponding phrase in Bach's chorale prelude is this:

J. S. Bach

Once again, the piece is in two unequal parts, both marked to be repeated. One sometimes hears an organist, at the repeat of the first part, play something like this:

It is quite clear what is happening. The organist is applying to Bach's melodic line the same process that Bach applied to the melody of the hymn tune. But no version corresponding to our third one here has ever been published. It is simply assumed that Bach is saying, "You see what I do; go on and do more of it for yourself."

Another example of the same principle is the *cadenza*, a strictly eighteenth-century provision for individual invention. By the time when concertos (chiefly violin concertos) were beginning to proliferate in the eighteenth century, the cult of the virtuoso musician was fairly established.[1] It was regarded as a judicious compliment to the soloist to provide

---

[1] The *concerto* was not originally a work for solo instrument and orchestra, but a work in a special style for orchestra alternating with a small group of instruments. Those which Bach wrote for solo instruments are among the earliest of their kind, and were to some extent imitations of the style of Vivaldi. But none of Bach's famous "Brandenburgs" is for solo instrument and orchestra, nor are Handel's *Concerti Grossi*.

in each movement a musical space which he would fill up with a solo that showed his skill. The soloist would in turn pay a compliment to the composer by improvising his solo on the themes which the movement had already stated. Traditionally the *cadenza*-space was provided between the last note but two and the last note but one of the soloist's part—at the "cadence" (hence its name). In classical concertos the orchestra might play a few summary bars at the end, but the soloist's part finished with the last note of his cadenza. The tradition was to improvise the cadenza; instrumentalists later tended to write their own rather than extemporize them, and sometimes a later composer might write a cadenza for an earlier composer's concerto (as Beethoven did for Mozart); later still, the composer would write one for his own concerto, as Rachmaninoff did. Brahms dispenses with cadenzas altogether in his piano concertos, and in any case the fully composed cadenza causes the listener to lose sight of the original purpose of the exercise, which was to suspend the composer's organization of effect, and to give the instrumentalist a chance to make his personal contribution to it.

3. Continuo

Arising out of this, we may bring in evidence the conventions of *continuo* playing from figured bass. Any pianist-reader of these pages who has any experience of accompanying eighteenth century works for violin or other instruments and *continuo* will have memories of unspeakable musical tedium. Nothing is more soul-destroying than to have to accompany on the piano some violin sonata by Handel, or any music of that kind, from a modern edition which is some hack musician's conscientious reconstruction of the *continuo* part. The reason is quite simple. The *continuo* part in eighteenth century music is a background part for a keyboard instrument designed to be improvised according to a harmonic pattern indicated by numerals added to a single bass line of music. You need only to hear a "realization" of a Purcell continuo part by Benjamin Britten to show how stimulating an experience the accompaniment of such music can be. The *continuo* player was expected to make his own music—never to obtrude it, but certainly never to leave it dull and lifeless. He was never provided with a full score by his composer; he was expected to do what was required by the soloist or small orchestra he was accompanying, and within the necessary limits of neighborliness, to make his own music.

4. Romantic versus Baroque

Before leaving this subject, we may for a moment return to Bach for another illustration, which is perhaps the most interesting of them all. Most people with any knowledge of music know that there has been a revolution in the interpretation of the organ music of Bach. In the history of this development of interpretation we have, incidentally, a handy example of our "Emotion—Knowledge—Will" pattern, though this is not my purpose in bringing it up here.

Following the example of Albert Schweitzer, who first popularized this form of interpretation forty years ago, the modern organist differs completely from his grandfather in his approach to Bach's music. Very roughly and untechnically described, the Schweitzer approach to Bach demands a use of the organ which subordinates everything to *clarity*, whereas the approach against which he reacted gave the primacy to a contrived effect on the listener. The pure Schweitzerian technique (to introduce a trifle of technicality) forbade the changing of registration during the course of a piece, and demanded such registration as would, at the expense of dramatic effects, make every note in Bach's counterpoint audible.

To understand the relevance of this one has to remember that although Bach was an early eighteenth-century composer, so far as the general listener is concerned, he did not appear as a recognized composer in the musical world until the mid-nineteenth century. And even then it was nothing like his whole output that was regarded as approachable enough to be included in ordinary concert programs. In other words, Bach broke upon the musical world when the romantic movement was at its height. Apart from the professionals and academics, Bach was appreciated by the public of those days as though he were a romantic composer; and indeed he had to wait until the early days of the present century before he achieved anything better than the specialized recognition of the musical elite.

The kind of thing that happened when Bach began to become popular was the presentation of a few of his works as highly dramatic, emotion-provoking pieces. Stokowski and Henry Wood both orchestrated the *Toccata and Fugue in D minor;* Stokowski added other pieces (notably the E-flat minor Prelude from Book I of the "Forty-eight" and the chorale preludes, "I call upon thee" and "We all believe in one God"); Elgar orchestrated the *Fantasia and Fugue in C minor,* and Respighi (with what now seems to be unbelievable vulgarity) the organ *Passacaglia.* Concert pianists brought the organ works into their repertory through arrangements by Liszt and Busoni. Dame Myra Hess in her piano arrangements of "Jesu, joy of man's desiring" and certain other cantata pieces produced highly popular piano pieces on a smaller scale. And of course there was always the "Air on the G String."

This is not in any sense to offer a puristic frown for those who arrange Bach's works for instruments for which he did not write them. He did it himself; there is nothing inherently wrong in doing this. What this tendency illustrates, however, is the desire among the arrangers to show nonspecialist listeners how great Bach was and how attractive his music is. Historical associations give way completely before the necessity to evoke a pleasurable response in the listener. And by the same token, the organists of 1920 were playing Bach's organ music as though it had been arranged for organ from an orchestral score, with all the dramatic aids for effect that the romantic organ could produce.

This was as typical of the age of emotion as was Schweitzer's demand that Bach's music must be so played as to sound as it would have sounded in Bach's own day. With typical historical enthusiasm, organists were encouraged to find out exactly how Bach's organs were tonally constructed, and what precisely Bach's ornaments meant, and to renounce all modern aids for effect that proved to be anachronistic. (The tremulant, for example, was not proscribed, because Bach had one on his organ; but the mechanical aids to stop changing on modern organs were forbidden because Bach's organ was in this respect primitive.)

The third stage is that which we illustrated under section one above: the attempt to re-create the true inventiveness and inspiration of Bach's musical ethos in a climate from which the intrusive emotionalism of the romantic age has been removed.

But the point here is this: Bach left no instructions about all this. The whole "baroque" debate on not only the playing of Bach but the construction of organs is a debate about interpretation. It has proved immensely fruitful, especially

now that organists, retreating from the extremes of pedantry, are willing to distinguish between the occasions when
Bach requires purity and asceticism in interpretation and
those when, had he had a modern organ at his disposal, he
would have quite certainly used everything it has to offer
in the way of effect-producing apparatus.[2] There are no
controversies of this kind in the interpretation of Schubert
or Beethoven or Mozart. But Bach at all levels is in himself
the case against any rigid textual fundamentalism in music.

5. Textual Criticism

Finally, to complete the case, consider what has been
learned during the hundred years of the modern antiquarian
revival (another movement which has passed very clearly
through the "Emotion—Knowledge—Will" pattern of
phases). I have referred in my book, *The English Carol*[3]
to the delightful history of the first systematic notation of
some of our best known carols. Pioneers like Davies Gilbert
and William Sandys, followed by more skillful technicians
like Lucy Broadwood and Cecil Sharp, collected carols,
words, and music, from people who sang them as the end
products of oral tradition. The attempts of Sandys to note
down what he heard from the rustics of the English West
Country are such as to give us no confidence at all that

---

[2] For example, let us take the Toccata in D minor and its associated Fugue (S. 565). It is perfectly clear that whereas the Fugue
is a simple and modest essay in counterpoint, the Toccata from its beginning to the end of the contrapuntal section before the final page of
rhetoric, is a stylized improvisation. It is designed to "show off" or "try
out" the organ—to see how much noise it will make, what the reverbera-
tion time of the building is, how fast its action will speak, and how aptly
its different tonal departments contrast with one another. The kind of
thing any organist does in testing an unfamiliar instrument is simply
"written up" in the Toccata. Any kind of "ascetic" treatment of it is as
unhistorical as is the "romantic" treatment of the Fugue.

[3] (New York: Oxford University Press, 1959.)

what he heard he communicated with any accuracy. It is no use asking: What is the correct version of "The First Noel"? (**Fig. 9**) and then expecting to get the authoritative and definitive answer from the first person who wrote the tune on paper—in this case Davies Gilbert:

Fig. 9 The First Noel

The first No - el the an. - gel did say was to cer - tain poor shep-herds in fields where they lay: in fields where they lay keep - ing their sheep on a cold win - ter's night that was so deep.

Similarly, we cannot be sure which version of "A Virgin Unspotted" (**Fig. 10, A–C**) is authentic; we know that Sandys' version cannot be right because it is obviously wrongly barred:

Fig. 10 A Virgin Unspotted

but even if we sing it like this (as some older carol books print it):

we may not be singing it rightly because Davies Gilbert
noted it like this:

20th-century carol books

C

But two different people in Cornwall very probably sang
it differently. The widespread preference today for the
Davies Gilbert version (version C) is the product of the
"Knowledge" phase of folk-song collecting; for whereas the
tendency in the older days was to note down and publish
what sounded easiest and most like a nineteenth-century
tune, the tendency in the later stage was to regard as authentic whatever sounded most unusual, and to publish and
approve whatever sounded most outlandish. (The "Will"
form of folk song is now fully operative; alongside the revival
of old songs, folk singers are now strenuously composing
new ones topical to the present age.)

Fig. 11   Angelus ad Virginem

1918   Gray (Oxford Book of Carols 52)
Slow

A

1950   Nicholson (Hymns Ancient and Modern, Revised 547)†

B

†Reprinted with permission of the Faith Press, Ltd.

1961   Routley (University Carol Book 8)

C

1965   Poston (Penguin Carol Book 1)*
Vivace

D

*Reprinted with permission of Penguin Books, Ltd.

Interesting variations on this theme occur when it is a matter of actually transcribing a manuscript written in a notation now unfamiliar. Take for example the delightful carol, "*Angelus ad Virginem*"—a carol rediscovered during the past 100 years from a manuscript in Dublin thought to date from about 1360. A glance at **Fig. 11** will show four successive attempts to reconstruct this carol: the first, by Alan Gray, appeared in *English Carol Book* (1918) and the first edition of the *Oxford Book of Carols* (1928); the second, by Sir Sydney Nicholson, appeared in *Hymns Ancient and Modern* (1950); the third, based on the second, is in the *University Carol Book* (1961); and the fourth is in the *Penguin Book of Christmas Carols* (1965), edited by Elizabeth Poston and based on a definitive version by Dom Anselm Hughes. There is a very elaborate version by Sir Richard Terry in his *Medieval Carol Book* (1931), now out of print. All these versions in their day claimed some measure of "authenticity." But it will be seen that it is largely a matter of interpretation—and it will be seen how far that interpretation was influenced by prevailing pressures of a nonmusical kind. All four versions make a very pleasant sound in their own way. Alan Gray's is strictly ecclesiastical, as if the transcriber were saying, "Carols are serene and beautiful; this is what that manuscript meant to convey." Equally, Elizabeth Poston shows in her version a trace of her anti-ecclesiastical approach, expressed with great emphasis in the preface to her collection. It is, in her day, good scholarship to emphasize the "outdoor" nature of carols and to interpret them in a manner as far removed as possible from the conventional church hymn. This begins to arouse doubts about the objectiveness and definitiveness of transcriptions claiming the highest scholarship. It is not as if Gray's version appeared in a romantic and anti-scholarly collection. But we all agree that now it won't do, and the 1964 edition of the *Oxford Book of Carols* included among its very few alterations a new version of this carol tune. Fundamentalism may be subjective; but so may the cult of the "original." Who knows exactly what contradictions of the "best scholarship" of today another age will bring?

Another example of transcription, this time showing a perfectly evident fault in understanding, is the very fine Christmas tune, *Divinum Mysterium*, sung to "Of the Father's love begotten." In **Fig.** 12 we give once again four versions. The first is the first version printed in England of a tune that was taken by its editor from a Finnish book, *Piae Cantiones*, dated 1582; the date of the transcription is 1853, and the transcriber is a musical antiquarian, Thomas Helmore. He is a characteristic mixture of the romantic and the pedagogue. He, with many other priest-musicians of his time, was an enthusiast for the revival of old music—in this he is a forerunner of the "Knowledge" age. But he has not yet the scholarly equipment to read the old notation, and the result he produces (still printed in the Standard edition of *Hymns Ancient and Modern*) is not only now known to be far from the intention of the original scribe, but, what matters more to our present argument, unsingable. In our example we have taken the fifth and sixth of the seven phrases of the tune for demonstration because they best illustrate the difficulties the transcribers were up against. Helmore's version, anyhow, never became popular. Nobody except a very in-group scholar talked of "that fine Christmas tune *Divinum Mysterium*" in 1900, because nobody knew it.

Vaughan Williams printed our second version in the *English Hymnal*, and got much nearer the spirit of the original (as we now think it must have been); but he

is usually thought to have gone astray at the one point at
which his version differs from version C: when he came
to revise his hymn book in 1933, he adopted version C,
which first gained currency in the 1904 edition of *Hymns
Ancient and Modern*, a book which was in preparation
while he was producing the *English Hymnal*, and which
has nothing in common with it.

Version A is the work of one who says "the old 1582
source had some good *hymns* in it"; doggedly he sets down
what he thinks the original must have meant, and he is
content that those who find it awkward and unintelligible
shall be as the philistines who know no better. It is version
C that has "caught on" in Britain—although it is perhaps
only since about 1945 that it has become anything like
generally known.

Fig. 12   Divinum Mysterium

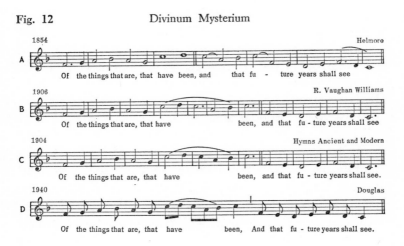

But what of version D, which Winfred Douglas used in
The Hymnal, 1940, of the Episcopal Church in the USA?

A glance at the original manuscript [4] shows that whatever
the 1582 source meant, it did not mean a tune in equal
notes. Quite clearly at least two note values are called for,
longs and shorts, and triple time is the obvious conjecture.
But Winfred Douglas knew that. What he also knew was
that the 1582 source was not by any means the original. It
was old enough for Helmore—270 years is a good historical
leap for an antiquarian of the mid-nineteenth century. But
the 1582 book was itself a transcription. What is more, it
was often a rendering into dance meters of tunes deriving
from plainsong. Douglas, then, says, "Let us restore the
plainsong form," and gives us the form in Version D, which
he conjectures to come from as far back as the twelfth
century.

So Helmore is bad transcription of 1582; Vaughan
Williams, corrected, is a good transcription of 1582. Douglas is a good transcription of something much earlier. If it
is antiquity you want, your vote goes to Douglas. If you
prefer Vaughan Williams, nothing in the world can prevent
your singing it and enjoying it, and at least it is a good
rendering of an old, if not an original, source. Helmore
is "out" anyway, because nobody ever wanted to sing him.
He is pedagogy without even knowledge, let alone any
sense of congregational attractiveness.

Scholars can be fundamentalists. That is the point. And
the truth that must never be lost sight of is that fundamentalism—the worship of written sources—makes no kind
of sense until it has connected with human life as everybody is in a position to observe it.

By now it will be evident that communication between
composer and audience, or from composer via performer

---

[4] It can be seen in a very careful transcription, preserving the old nota-
tional form, in G. R. Woodward's edition of *Piae Cantiones*, published by
the Plainsong & Medieval Music Society of Great Britain in 1910, no. XX.

to audience, for composer, via editor to reader, is a process which has a good deal in common with the communication of Christian truth through the Scriptures. Both the Scriptures and music are a more complex critical subject than most people recognize. Even before we take any account of non-European music (for example the jazz tradition), we can see that literalism is an unsafe guide. We can also see that even claims to authenticity and scholarship are rarely, if ever, made by people who are entirely immune from the pressures of surrounding opinions and tendencies of thought.[5]

[5] There are other exercises in musical paleography which through the disagreement of transcribers have produced parallel and conflicting versions of current tunes. There is the carol, "In dulci jubilo," which may be compared with the version of the tune usually sung to Neale's paraphrase, "Good Christian men, rejoice" (on which see *The English Carol*, p. 196); or there is the tune to "Unto us a boy is born"—again from *Piae Cantiones*, but transcribed there in one way, and in another (in triple time) by Praetorius in 1610—see *Hymnal*, 1940, 34 and 47, for the two versions.

4. the defect of fundamentalism

The Music-Lover's Orthodoxy

The examples at the end of the last chapter were designed to show that the authority in a musical text is not always easy to establish, and therefore that not all forms of music depend on the kind of authority which resides in the text of a classical work. The time has clearly come now to turn to the world of jazz music. I refer to it here simply as another illustration of the complexity of the problem of authority in music; other aspects of it must be dealt with at a later stage. In the world of jazz nowadays there is a folk element and also a professional element. As folk music, jazz is subject to all the organizational anarchy that folk music is content to bear. Its religious and social origins ensure that it becomes a folk music that is as near to prophetic ecstasy—typical yet escapist, earthy yet aspiring, crude yet haunting—as are the Negro spirituals in which it has its musical roots. The "inspirational" content of jazz has a close affinity with the singing and dancing of the ancient Israelite prophets—much closer than any it has with conventional European music. Jazz in its cultured forms makes room for the inspirational variation, the cadenza, the wild *ex tempore* utterance confined rigidly within the primitive rhythmic and harmonic framework. In jazz the principle of authority is firm enough—in the unvarying pattern within which the improvisation is invited to occur; and the essence of this kind of music is the violent strife between the discipline of the pattern and the freedom of the inspiration.

The Challenge of Jazz

Jazz, indeed, has some remote affinity with eighteenth-century European convention—we have observed already (p. 61, example 8 above) the conventions of free variation and of cadenza in the music of Bach's time. But what jazz has no affinity whatever with is the totally controlled effect of romantic concert music.

It is true that jazz "composition" has been an inevitable accompaniment of the professionalizing of jazz. There has been plenty of experiment with jazz rhythms in music of the accepted "concert" kind, since Constant Lambert's historic experiment in 1929 with *The Rio Grande*. The jazz idiom has proved to be infinitely adaptable, and it has bound together a whole musical culture which now ranges from primitive forms to a music of subtlety and seriousness sufficient to hold the attention of listeners and critics who are entirely conditioned by the romantic musical assumptions of Europe.

But when we bring jazz into an argument about church music, what are we doing? Are we adding one more clause to the argument that church music is not essentially fundamentalist, not tied to one single assumption about authority? We cannot bring it as evidence toward that conclusion until we have shown in what sense jazz music is relevant to the church at all. This we cannot do without offering some argument against prevailing assumptions and prejudices. I ask the reader to wait a little for this—for

I have something later to say on this matter, but it would be too large a digression to be suitable at this point. If we are content for the present just to remember that jazz has an unquestionably religious origin and to concede religious authority to the spirituals from which it came, we can suspend judgment about its use in modern church life.

The conclusion toward which I want to press without further digression at present is this: that until we have recast our assumptions about authority within music, we shall not fully understand what church music is, or how to judge it and use it.

And even if we leave jazz out of the argument, we can see that in ordinary practice church music is not limited to the kind of music that the music-lover normally thinks of as serious, or classical music. Jazz is merely the most familiar and alarming contemporary kind of music that defies fundamentalism. It is pentecostal rather than dogmatic. The church therefore, in one of its moods, ought to be profoundly interested in it. But let us return to the more familiar ground of current church practice.

Standards

Let us consider what we often hear referred to as "standards"; let us consider the kind of aspirations at which they aim at the Royal School of Church Music or at the Westminster Choir College. I have no intention whatever of undermining the authority or disparaging the aims of these excellent institutions. All I ask here is what is their place in the total scheme of Christian music-making, and all I need to apologize for is resisting the notion that they are themselves the whole of that scheme.

In pursuit of their aims, these and all other academies of the Western church music culture seek to inculcate high standards of church music. The choirmasters they educate turn into men who seek to train their choirs in the exact yet inspired interpretation of church music from Dunstable to Britten and beyond. The instruction that the choirmaster gives his choir insists on faithful observance of the text. The requirements he makes of his publisher include that of good editions of old music that make authentic interpretations possible, by spelling out the shorthand and codifying the assumed conventions of the older writers. His choice of music is more and more critical, indicating an increasing demand for the highest integrity in composers. Of his singers he demands a pure and disciplined tone, a sensitive ear, a rhythmic awareness, and a readiness to learn first to be obedient to the composer and the conductor ("Watch the *beat!*" "Mind the *rests!*") and then to fill in the pattern of obedience with personal commitment and inspiration. In this way our best choirs can now be relied on to sing demonstrably good music demonstrably well. They achieve this by learning not to sing what they think is there, but what is there on the paper. (My own choirmaster's favorite expression to his singers is, "Don't *compose*; sing what's written!") The division of labor between composer, conductor, and performer is as complete and well defined as it is when a pianist is playing the *Hammerklavier*. When we sing Purcell we get hold of Watkins Shaw's edition; when we sing Gibbons we go to Fellowes and Thurston Dart; when we sing fifteenth-century music we go to Denis Stevens, and the purpose of these editors is to help us produce an authentic effect by following instructions which the older composers did not give, but which we are used to getting from the later ones. A modern choir is not asked to interpret or improvise as was the eighteenth-century conductor or continuo player.

Now, it would be ridiculous to disparage this. This is the only way of doing this particular job. But this is not

the only job that church music has to do. In the days of
scholarship and research, stereo recordings and television
performances, traveling American choirs who bring great
distinction to English church music, and the flourishing of
institutions like the R.S.C.M. and Westminster and all the
church music schools which are the special glories of the
U.S.A., it is easy to forget that anything else has to happen
in church but choir music; but on the other hand the
sweeping social changes which in Britain have made it so
difficult for local church choirs to maintain their strength
have drawn our attention, at least in that country, to the
existence of other forms of church music and to the need
for a proper assessment of their place in the total scheme.

Ambiguous Moralities

I need hardly remind any reader of these pages of the
conflict which we so often hear about, arising between the
highly trained specialist musician in charge of the choir
music and the demands of a generalized congregation. That
conflict, whose resolution is difficult enough to become,
when it is achieved, a major pastoral victory, is the end
product of a basic disagreement about what music is. The
congregation regards its hymns as folk songs; the choir
and organist regard their music as serious music demanding
musical obedience. To the choir and organist a new piece
of music is in principle easy to learn because they have
learned the technique as well as the principle of obedience.
They know that they must read the notes, and they know
how to read them. By contrast, to the ordinary member
of the congregation, who is not a member of the congregation because he is a musician, there is something as incongruous in learning a new hymn tune as in learning a
new tune to "The First Noel" or "The Star-Spangled Ban-
ner." On the one side there are pedagogic standards, on the

other, the traditional folk-song standards. When one side says that a certain hymn tune is "not good enough," the other side says that this is unintelligible nonsense. What have goodness or badness to do with it?

Or consider the occasional well-known hymn which, in the view of a musician, congregations constantly sing incorrectly—for example, the interpolated note just before the refrain in "O come, all ye faithful" (**Fig. 13**), or the sixth line of the tune "Austria" (**Fig. 14**):

Fig. 13   O Come, All Ye Faithful

Fig. 14   Austria

The organist has his hymnal, and he knows what the "right" notes are, and it worries him when congregations sing them "wrong." But what he often does not know is that in insisting that the version in his hymnal is "right" he is starting a philosophical discussion about the meaning of "right" which may land him in deep water. In the case of "O come, all ye faithful," for example, he will have either to be ignorant, or to suppress knowledge, of the fact that a very early version of that tune is in triple time.[1] Why is not *that* version "right"? In the case of "Austria" he may refer to Haydn's manuscript, but if he does, he will

[1] See the "Jacobite MS" reproduced in J. Stéphan, *Adeste Fideles* (Buckfast Abbey, England, 1947).

probably receive one or two surprises. (Unfortunately the manuscript seems to have perished.)

No, this argument will not really hold. What the choirmaster who is trying to handle an unbiddable congregation ought to say is, "We must have some unanimity about this, for our purposes, we shall assume that the version in the hymnal is 'right'; anyhow, that's what you must sing." The choirmaster will commit the cardinal error of fundamentalism if he says, "The hymnal version is right, always right, and unalterably right." He may only say "We are going to take this as right for *us*, because we'll have complete confusion if we don't agree on something."

Of course it is going to make for order and agreement in the church if hymnal editors will come to some sort of understanding about the versions they print (in fact some editors do print the interpolated note in "O come, all ye faithful" still); but that is a counsel of perfection, and quite possibly, if we admit that even the present year has not brought us to the age of perfection, a counsel of dullness.

But the wider issue behind that particular case is this: that congregational music, performed not by professionals, offered even to the tone-deaf as an opportunity for their participation in worship, is simply a different kind of music from choir music, or at any rate from the choir music we are at present familiar with in Western circles. The history of this cleavage is fascinating in itself; it is the history of the hymn tune. And so much of that history is a history of custom; a good deal of it is practically social anthropology. (At any rate, you cannot be a tolerable hymnologist without having some interest in sociology.) It includes such episodes as the extraordinary story of the so-called "Bach chorale." (Bach once more comes in to confound our generalizations.) In Bach's arrangements of old Lutheran tunes for congregational singing in his cantatas and passions (not in liturgical worship), you have example after example of the master hand in editorial work; Bach takes the old tunes and makes them accessible to the ears of eighteenth-century Lutherans by making radical alterations, substituting rich harmony and dance rhythm for the bare unison and flexible rhythm of the originals. And in his own corner of heaven Johann Sebastian is no doubt laughing heartily at our current controversies—especially to be heard among modern Lutherans—as to whether the Bach versions or the original versions are the "right" versions. Bach brought the "old tunes" back to people who, infected by operatic dance styles, had forgotten them; he brought them back by making them sound like their kind of music. He did it magnificently. He would not have done it at all had he not been thinking primarily of ordinary people joining in the singing of his great church works.

There are, then, certain points where pedantry is a necessity, and certain others where it is entirely irrelevant, in church. It is precisely right in training a choir; in dealing with a congregation it can be as incongruous as using a 4,000 horsepower engine to push a baby carriage.

The Organist's Guilty Secret

There is one man who is plumb in the center of this controversy, and that is the organist, who in an ordinary congregation must spend some of his time practicing the utmost pedantry, in playing his voluntaries and training his choir, and who must spend another part of his time accompanying a general congregation singing Old Hundredth or "For all the saints." A good church organist ought to be one of the most cultivated, humane, well-rounded musicians alive, for it is given to few to practice in equal proportions the virtues of obedience and of invention as it is given to him. Unhappily he is too often (in Britain anyhow) regarded as the meanest of musicians, and too seldom extolled in terms of the richness of his calling, for it to occur to him that in many ways he is a great deal better off than a first-class concert pianist. But consider what in fact he has to do, or can regard himself as having to do. He has the opportunity of playing solos before a regular audience. The fact that most of them do not listen has nothing to do with the fact that if he plays the "Great" E minor Fugue of Bach as an outgoing voluntary, or one of the Preludes from the Klavierübung as in incoming one, he can, if he will, play them at the standard which a concert-pianist demands of himself. He has also the duty of accompanying the choir—which means either playing a composed organ accompaniment of some intricacy by Benjamin Britten, or playing a Brahms or Parry accompaniment from a piano score, or reconstituting an orchestral accompaniment reduced to piano score—three very different techniques in themselves. Then beyond this he has to keep a singing congregation happy and be prepared to improvise intelligibly for liturgical purposes. If he is especially fortunate he may have also to accompany plainsong—which those who do it well regard as one of the most delightful of all organistic disciplines.

The fact is, however, that in nine tenths of the anthems he accompanies, and in all hymn tunes whatever, the player has to arrange for the organ what has been written for some other instrument, or for voices. Most hymn tunes are written for four voices; a few have an accompaniment written out as for a piano, but I have never seen one with a three-staff organ accompaniment. Playing the famous "How lovely" from Brahms's *Requiem*, the organist has to reconstitute an orchestral score written out in a piano arrange-

ment. The decision-content in the organist's work, so far
as it is within the church service, is far greater than that
required of any other musician except the jazz soloist.

I may add that the organist who plays hymns for a congregation so that the people really enjoy singing them has
a large variety of techniques at his command and makes
many decisions on his individual initiative. These include
choosing the appropriate registration for the announcement and the different verses, anticipating the correct
tempo, and even, in places, varying the harmony. Few
people realize that the organist is composing nearly all
the time he is at the console for a church service. The pattern he follows when playing the plain text of a hymn tune
is exactly that of the eighteenth-century continuo player
who improvised an accompaniment within the strict limits
of the harmony prescribed in the score. It is the same with
plainsong—but here he has a unison melody which must
be accompanied within the pattern laid down by the mode
of the tune. The essence of organ playing for a congregation is the combination of the alert and neighborly sensitiveness which places the player in rapport with the singers
with an inspirational freedom which enables him to trans-
figure what would otherwise have been a routine affair.[2]

In these highly professionalized days, then, it needs to
be emphasized that church music contains a good deal of
activity that is not on all fours with the music that the

[2] I am aware that there is some controversy in organistic circles about
the propriety of varying harmonies in those verses of hymns where the
voices sing in unison. Some believe that it is illegitimate. All I can say
is that I have heard it done often enough with restrained excellence, and
without any sign of the congregation's being thrown off course, to hold
the view that, done in a musicianly way, it is a perfectly legitimate adornment of hymn singing. It should not be necessary to say that if it is done
for vulgar display it will be as offensive as anything else done for that
purpose in worship; and that if it is done in an unmusicianly way it is as
incongruous as anything else done badly in worship would be.

concertgoer appreciates. The church is a place were people who are not musicians sing, and where the gifts of the musician can be used in a pastoral fashion as well as in the normally accepted professional fashion. On this subject I have moralized enough in other places to be able here to leave it at that.[3] The conclusion of this present argument is that a fundamentalist attitude to music imposes unwarrantable limitations on a proper judgment of church music in our time.

Fundamentalism

Need I apologize for "fundamentalist"? I think that the sense in which I am using it is legitimate, and that it will already have become clear. I take the fundamentalist to be, in church music, the man who places too much faith in a written text, and uses that text as an excuse for not asking critical questions that it is legitimate to ask.

Certain kinds of music, we have said, demand a rigorous adherence to a written text, and therefore a certain kind of obedience in the performer. But many other kinds do not. Church music, we have further said, includes music, and musical activities, of these other kinds. I am about to say that the recognition of this could so liberate church music as to enable it to provide new kinds that would answer the current complaint that church music is unduly conservative and socially selective.

If I may now refer back to certain earlier arguments, I hold that it is the same kind of error which says that Helmore's version of *Divinum Mysterium* is the correct one, which also says that the King James Version of the Scriptures is inerrantly inspired. In both cases it is possible to take a passage which strictly does not make sense and

---

[3] See *Church Music and Theology* (Philadelphia: Fortress Press, 1960) and *Music, Sacred and Profane* (London: Independent Press, 1960).

say, none the less for that, that it is "right" or "inspired."
The distorted phrase two thirds of the way through Helmore's *Divinum Mysterium* (see **Fig. 12, A**) is the same
kind of misleading interpretation as "and not increased
the joy" in Isaiah 9:3 (where "not" is a mistranslation),
or as "Search the scriptures" in John 5:39 (where an im-
perative has been substituted for an indicative—"You
search").

Similarly, to take a folktale like Genesis 3 and interpret
it literally is like trying to find an authentic version of "The
First Noel," or saying that the version we know is "right."
because most people know it. It does not happen to matter
two straws whether our version of "The First Noel" is right
or "wrong," because it does not matter to anybody but a
historian what "The First Noel" sounded like when it was
first sung. In the same way, it matters to nobody whether
the first man was or was not called "Adam," although no
doubt if anybody ever does discover what the first man's
name was, it will be very interesting. Moreover, if anybody
discovers that the first man's name was not "Adam" but
something else, it will not make the least difference in
the moral import of the story about him. (By the same
token, the theory put forward recently by certain experimenters who have used a computer to determine which of
the so-called Pauline Epistles were written by Paul [4] makes
no difference to the authority which the church should
ascribe to what is written in those letters. I disagree with
the authors of these experiments at that point without
questioning the validity of their findings.)

It is familiar to scholars and students of the Bible that
over-romantic, over-pedantic, and over-existential interpretations of the biblical texts have all led to errors. In the

[4] See A. Q. Morton and McLeman, *Christianity and the Computer*
(London: Hodder & Stoughton, 1964).

first place, it is illegitimate to confine, in practice, one's obedience to those passages of Scripture which sound most like writings that could have been written in one's own time, or which through the accidental beauty of their translations we find memorable. Isaiah 40 has a beautiful rhythm, and so has psalm 23, and so has I Corinthians 13, so we find them especially memorable and therefore especially authoritative. The "Sermon on the Mount" contains so much moral teaching that we wish others would follow, that we ascribe special, and often quite unintended, authority to it above the other recorded sayings of Jesus. This is romantic—making the Bible sound like a book of our own time. In the second place, it is possible to be so pedantic about sources as to discourage all inspiration and all ascription of authority to it. Some scholars behave as though the Bible has nothing to say to anybody who does not know not only Hebrew but also Akkadian. In the third place, it is possible to produce translations and new interpretations so zealous for communication that while they "make the Bible live" to the hearer, one can never be sure that it is the Bible that is being made to live.

Let all that be admitted; it is still true that the most widespread error is that of selecting a few passages from Scripture and according to them an authority that is bound wholly by the English text. Fundamentalism has been called the cult of the Epistle to the Romans. In its most pernicious form it is undoubtedly the cult of a very small section of the Bible (broken up into uncontexted and therefore misleading quotations). The most dazzling of fundamentalist preachers may bemuse his hearers by quoting twenty or thirty biblical texts in his sermon and still show no evidence that he has approached the heart of the Bible or has any doctrine of biblical authority beyond

what may be crudely expressed in the proposition, "The
bits of the Bible I quote are authoritative."

If we are learning—taught by the various schools of
biblical criticism from form critics to demythologists—
that the authority of the Bible is more complex than fundamentalism allows, then we are learning to be human.
We need to learn the same about music. Music is not doing
what the Bible does, and therefore there is no question
here of moral danger in misinterpretation. But at the practical level, the level of day-to-day decision, our judgment
is going to be very seriously clouded if we go on thinking
that good music is music which is interpreted by the letter
of the score, and therefore that church music need develop
only in the direction which has been taken by "music-
lover's music" since about 1800. I have pointed out that
modern experimental music, jazz music, and ordinary commonplace church music all defy that assumption. I shall
now turn to a quite different argument that leads us a
stage further toward our ultimate goal.

III
assault on conformity

5. the urge to conform

The Christian church is a society. One of the special marks of our present age is the church's concern with the question of how it is related to that other society which is humanity —society as expressed in a limited community (a race, a nation, a city), or society at large. It is high time that the current enthusiasm for sociology found expression in the field of music, and especially time that somebody attempted to do for church music what Wilfred Mellers has been doing for music in general in his books (especially *Man and His Music*). There are many practical problems in church music whose solution must wait until it has been generally recognized that musicians and Christians are all men. G. K. Chesterton's best joke was in the opening lines of an essay, where he began, "The human race, to which so many of my readers belong. . . ." There is a certain mournful irony in the thought that so many theologians are still prepared to regard musicians as exceptions to humanity, and that so many musicians reciprocate the assumption toward theologians.

The Proud Piano
I want to enter on this part of my argument by referring to one of the most cheerful attempts to give us a bird's-eye view of musical sociology—Arthur Loesser's book, *Men, Women and Pianos*. This is a social history—exhaustive,

anecdotal, and often intensely entertaining—of the most socially revealing of all technical developments in music, namely, the rise, enthronement, and fall of the piano. I would recommend the book to anybody who can read, whether he is musical or not. Here is a passage from one of its later chapters.

The piano can be seen as a feature in the physiognomy of a certain way of life, the way of moneyed middle-class people, of the bourgeoisie, whose habits dominated the Western world for a century and a half. In the middle eighteenth century, when these people first felt their importance and their strength, they believed mystically in liberty, in unrestrained expression in word and tone, and in the emphatic utterance of humane sentiment: thus they wanted an instrument that could play any tone loud or soft from bodily impulse at the whim of an instant, that could reflect the free, incalculable play of "feeling" within their hearts. They believed in "humanity," in the right of all human beings, regardless of their birth, to an opportunity for their self-development: therefore they compelled their children to take music lessons, and thus they favored the piano—on which even the most slow-handed and dull-eared could produce some minimum of acceptable result. The liberty they prized the most was the liberty to engage in lucrative schemes, to pile up profits: they believed in money and in the palpable evidences of its assured possession, and that gave them a predilection for an instrument that looked solid and expensive in a drawing-room. Their belief in business enterprise allowed them to think of music as a simple article of commerce, and thus to encourage publishers to put out vast quantities of music that wallowed in identical formulas, so as to keep up a steady stream of buying and selling. They agreed with Rousseau that woman exists only with reference to man, and for his comfort and vanity, and that her place is in the home; thus they liked an instrument that she could play congruously with her aspect of chaste idleness. Presently they developed a great admiration for what they could, with some superstitious exaggeration, call individual achievement. They spun dreams about bold, crazy heroes; and they enjoyed looking up worshipfully—especially after his defeat and departure—to one man who could rise from artillery captain to European dictator, or to another who could climb from antique-peddler to world banker: thus they liked to expend their hero-worship upon piano-virtuosos whose startling feats of loudness, speed, and agility commanded the attention of thousands, and who, humbly born, came to have their names linked with those of princesses. They believed in mechanical devices, which helped them to make more money; and that gave them affection for an instrument that had many moving parts. They believed in the iron of their steam engines and did not shrink from introducing its severity into their pianos, so that the virtuosos could play still louder without smashing them.[1]

That comes from the book's conclusion; but I can assure the reader that its earlier chapters, there summarized, are devastatingly documented. The piano is here shown to be the culture symbol of romanticism—of its titanism, its individualism, and its preoccupation with present sensations. It is exactly the instrument of what we, following Tillich, are calling the culture of Emotion.

The Unsociable Piano

Let us then ponder the implications of this. We might begin by noting in what ways the piano as a musical instrument has puzzled the composers once they began to have a suspicion that there was more to it than met the romantic ear. Note how in the hands of romantic composers the piano is an expressive instrument, given to the exploitation of its variety of tone impact—the brilliance

[1] *Men, Women and Pianos* (New York: Simon and Schuster, 1954), pp. 607-8.

of its upper registers for the bravura passage-work of Chopin and Liszt, the unrivaled possibilities for *cantabile* in Schubert and Schumann, the sonority of the bass in widespread *arpeggio* writing in Brahms, the faculty for sudden *sforzando* and piled up, furious *fortissimo* in Beethoven. Contrast all this with the increasingly primitive and percussive use of the instrument that post-romantics like Bartok insist on, and follow the story until you meet electronic composers who tape-record piano tones in vibrations, or make use of small sections of the complex of quick rise and slow fall in volume that is produced from a piano string struck while the dampers are off. The history of recent piano writing (in a way, it almost begins with Brahms) is the story of composers' struggle to get free of the piano's romantic associations either by making it once again a primitive instrument of percussion or by treating it as a product of modern technology pure and simple. There is often a piano in an avant-garde piece for live orchestra, but you would hardly recognize the piano in Boulez's *Pli Selon Pli* with the instrument that strives so majestically with the orchestra in a concerto by Rachmaninof.

The Antisocial Piano

This is a half-conscious social movement. Contemporary composers would not explain their experiments with the piano in just these terms, true and adequate though we claim this analysis to be. But we can confirm it by a more crudely social observation. What has happened to the piano as a piece of furniture, an adjunct of gracious living? In modern British society at any rate, the most obvious physical qualities about a piano are not its expensiveness (for any high quality musical instrument is expensive, and so is good quality hi-fi equipment, and anyhow the auto-

mobile has arrived as the most coveted status symbol); they
are rather, its size and the amount of noise it makes. Anybody who thinks it normal to have a piano in the
house and to play it with more than the most casual attention must think it normal to have a house with a room
large enough to accommodate it and standing far enough
from its neighbors for the sound not to be a social nuisance.
In the culture which regarded pianos as normal, these
things also were normal. Pianos in their heyday went
with spacious and well-built houses. They go ill with
blocks of flats with defective sound insulation, or with
small government-built houses on crowded estates. They
do not even go very well with mobility. The contemporary
substitute for the piano is not the radio or the television
but the guitar, a small portable instrument of thoroughly
respectable musical lineage which can be played adequately
without much trouble and which, unless it be connected
with an amplifier according to a regrettable modern custom,
makes a tolerably inoffensive and private noise. The piano
in its great days was the thing that Paderewski played—
it could tinkle or it could roar, but it really fitted the
style of life of those who could afford the space, as well as
the money, that it required.

I mention all this because I wish to go on to suggest
that those who are interested in the music or the church
nowadays are very often to be found among those for whom
the piano is still the central musical instrument. If we examine this assumption of the centrality of the piano, we
shall find that it is encrusted with certain social assumptions which it is probably time now to question.

The Lonely Piano

For example, contrast the kind of music which was felt
to be normal, whether inside or outside church, in the days

before there were pianos, with the sort of music so widely felt to be normal now in church (although its normality is being radically doubted outside the church). In the pre-piano days music was vocal: it was melodic, or contrapuntal (the same thing), and rhythmic. It was not in the nine-teenth-century sense *harmonic*. The traditional compass of the string band or the pre-piano keyboard corresponded roughly with the extremes attainable by a normal group of human voices. The use of the *chord* as a source of sensation in itself is a romantic custom. The rhetorical and evocative dissonances in Bach (or in Byrd) are always the by-products of a counterpoint which is basically vocal. Music for wind, or strings, or keyboard had a vocal basis. The recent records made by the Swingle Singers of music by Bach, Handel, and Mozart show how easily this instrumental music can be returned to the voice.

It would be fanciful to say that the piano was the *cause* of the romantic interest in instruments for their own sake. The point is that the piano symbolizes and gathers up in itself the breakout from vocal music that was the chief physical quality of romantic music. It had started before there were pianos. But the coming of the piano gave it the needed boost.

The secret is that the piano is instrumentally a thoroughly bad mixer. The piano is absolutely no use for eighteenth-century *continuo* work. Use an eighteenth-century "posi-tive" organ or a harpsichord, and the effect is of a perfect blend with strings or woodwind; you hardly hear the con-tinuo instrument, though you would sadly miss it if it were not present. Use a piano for the same work, and the piano tone never disappears from the center of the sound pattern. You feel, in a piece of any length, how pleasant it would be if that piano would stop murmuring and commenting—it is nearly as bad as intrusive whispers from the audience.

Romantic chamber music, of course, exploits this in-
alienable property of the piano. As soon as the piano trio,
quartet, or quintet gets into its stride as a musical form, the
composer uses his instruments to evoke characteristic notions of strife, conflict, and large-scale controversy. I would
in passing[2] draw attention again to the quite remarkable behavior of the piano in the piano trios and the *Trout* Quintet
of Schubert. In the *Trout*, where the piano is associated
with a rich-toned string combination (including double-
bass), the piano part is distinguished by hundreds of bars
of open octaves—effective as heard, but not what the piano
was designed for. In the Trios D 898 (B flat) and D 911
(E flat), there are many passages of piano writing better
than Schubert produces anywhere else—the whole of the
first movement of D 898, for example; but there are some
uneasy compromises: the majestic cello tune in the slow
movement of D 911 simply isn't a piano tune, and is very
difficult to bring off when the piano gets it—but it looks as
if the composer thought the piano must at all costs get its
share of what music was going, because he never gives this
archetypally "string" tune to the violin in that movement.
From Beethoven to Brahms the piano proved to be an
intractable and unbiddable instrument for chamber music;
pianists demanded it, so it got written, and the problems
it posed were not by any means beyond the genius of the
greatest of the romantic composers, whose intellectual
grasp of their subject was enough to carry them through
the practical difficulties. All the same, it is generally con-
ceded that the composers who wrote the finest piano
chamber works never produced the very greatest of their
work in this form: that can be checked by reference to the
chamber works that are regarded as the pinnacles of achievement in each case—Beethoven's posthumous string quar-

[2] See *Music, Sacred and Profane*, pp. 19-20.

tets, Mozart's string quartets and quintets (perhaps K 465
and K 516 at the top), Schubert's C major string quintet
and G major quartet, Mendelssohn's *Midsummer Night's
Dream*, and Brahms's Clarinet Quintet.

The piano is the instrument of individual present sensation. The greatness of romantic music was in its successful
acceptance of the heroic task of matching the new harmonic
force with equal intellectual demand—of transcending the
essential carnality of the piano. Once the tension snapped,
the collapse was catastrophic.

The Antivocal Piano

This is far from being irrelevant to church music. In the
pre-piano days, all church music is voice-centered. This is
true not only of the golden age of sixteenth-century
polyphony but of all music right up to Bach and his contemporaries. Even when it became florid and exuberant,
the genesis of the style was in opera, which is vocal. But
even in the old psalm tunes of just before and after 1600
one can see how voice-centered church music is. Psalm
tunes of the Genevan or old English and Scottish kind were
designed primarily for singing in unison and unaccompanied. But harmonized versions of them were printed for
domestic use, and some of the leading composers of the day
(such as Bourgeois and Goudimel in France, or Dowland,
Alison, and Kirbye in England) provided these harmoniza-
tions. They were sometimes in a simple madrigal style; they
were never instrumental in style, even if they were sometimes played on instruments in the homes where they were
sung. When one looks through Ravenscroft's edition of the
current psalm tunes in England (1621) it is not long before
one encounters something that no nineteenth-century editor would have dreamed of writing. Even allowing for the
change of convention which now puts the melody in the

treble part where in those days it was in the tenor, arrangements such as these that follow are typical sixteenth-century vocal music. Note, for example, the late entry of the bass at the beginning of "Dundee (French)" (**Fig. 15**), the syncopations in the fourth phrase of "Old Hundredth" (**Fig. 16**), and the constant crossing of parts in both tunes:

Fig. 15   Dundee (French)

Fig. 16   Old 100th

In a chorale arrangement by Bach, over a century later, we still have a strictly vocal technique, and even when eighteenth-century accompaniments to anthems suggest strings or woodwind, they never suggest the piano. What we are demonstrating here can hardly be better exemplified than in simply quoting a very characteristic "romantic" hymn tune of the nineteenth century—Joseph Barnby's tune to "Lord of our life and God of our salvation."

Fig. 17   Cloisters
                                                              J. Barnby

There is only one instrument that could have produced that musical style: the romantic piano. It is the piano that really exploits repeated sustained chords, accented dissonances, and melodies that do not depend on the breathing power of a human pair of lungs. Try arranging that tune for any combination of primitive instruments—strings, woodwind, brass—and sooner or later you come to a passage which must either sound ludicrous or be drastically re-scored. Even on the organ those repeated chords are difficult to make aurally pleasant. And as for the voice—what composer whose musical sense was voice-centered could combine all those repeated notes in the inner parts with that third phrase which so ruthlessly demands higher and higher notes as the breath runs out? We are here making no judgment about the quality of Barnby's tune as music, although it could plausibly be contended that as congregational folk song it leaves much to be desired. The point is that it, and indeed all that enormous family of hymn tunes that exploit repeated chords, is the consequence of nothing but the cult of the piano.

If the piano is an instrument that produces such impressive effects with such relatively small expenditure of effort, then it is the symbol—and its widespread use is the direct cause—of the collapse of romantic music with which in church we are so sadly familiar. That age of cheap aesthetic returns was also the age of cheap publishing, and the reason why church music is still so firmly wedded to nineteenth-century traditions is the enormous, the irresistible weight of music which that age caused to be composed for it. A habit so heavily stamped into the character of a community naturally dies hard.

The Organ Uneasily Enthroned

Now consider the development of the organ in English and American churches. In the sixteenth century the continental organ was a primitive instrument for accompaniment; the baroque organ of a century later was designed to render music that depended on counterpoint rather than on harmonic sensations (that is to say, it was voice-centered). The romantic organ, which for historical reasons was the first kind of organ heard at all widely in English churches, was designed to create an impression of majesty, grandeur, and remoteness.

Continental churches by 1850 all had organs, and organs often of extreme sophistication. Their authorities were little tempted to adjust these to romantic fashions, even when they were content that romantic music should be played on them. But the puritan ethos of the English churches—no less powerful among Anglicans than among Dissenters until about 1850—saw to it that the development of the organ was severely stunted. When that ethos, which was not so much opposed to music as scandalously neglectful of it, was eventually broken through by the protests of such musicians as Samuel Sebastian Wesley, the ground was clear for massive developments along what were then thoroughly contemporary lines. The archetypal large organ was that erected in the Crystal Palace in London's Hyde Park for the Great Exhibition of 1851; at that time few English cathedral organs had a full pedal board, and organ recitals were commoner in large contemporary Dissenting chapels than in Anglican churches. What with the success mystique of the Great Exhibition and the newfound enthusiasm for massive organs, all was set for the production of larger and larger, more and more sonorous, instruments, and for the organ to become known as the "King of Instruments." The idea of an organ that could not, when required, fill the building in which it was erected with a mass of sound that approached the limits of human endurance with nicely calculated vertiginous proximity would have seemed absurd to any organ builder of the time. If the piano could make a marvelously loud noise, the organ could do better. The limits of sonority and the limits of suggestive softness were alike within the compass of every normal church organ— and the fashion continues today. Along with this development of organs which suggested, in the manner of con-

temporary evangelists, immense power and also the capacity
for the tenderest and most erotic effects came a spate of
organ music of a triviality that matched well the incredible
vulgarity of music purveyed for amateur pianists. Apart
from Parry and Stanford—who wrote some of their best
work for the organ—the organ composers of 1900 are adequately represented by Alfred Hollins (1865-1942). His
work, composed almost entirely for the delectation of a congregation in Edinburgh which crowded a central church to
hear fashionable preachers denounce the sins of the flesh,
is as shamelessly (one is almost tempted to say innocently)
carnal as anything that came from the contemporary music-
hall stage.

It is only fair to add that around 1900 there was a decisive movement to rescue the organ from its bondage to
spiritual corruption. It could primarily be done only by recalling Bach, retracing one's steps, and starting out again.
This is what Parry did in his organ works, and to a certain
extent what Rheinberger did in the best movements of his
sonatas, such as the Prelude and Fugue from that in B
minor. One of Parry's best organ works well exemplifies
his debt to Bach and at the same time his command of the
romantic idiom—the Fantasia and Fugue in G major,
whose first movement is openly modeled on Bach's great
Fantasia in G minor, and whose second movement is as
good a romantic fugue as can be found anywhere. But organ
music has followed choral music in reproducing the three-
fold cultural pattern which we mentioned at the opening of
this book. For after a notable romantic revival in Parry,
Stanford, Rheinberger, and Reubke (with a contribution
from Elgar in his Sonata in G, and a whole library of
variously romantic work by Karg-Elert and Widor), a reaction toward a severer classicism has come in the work of
Flor Peeters and Pepping—more self-consciously Bach-like

(indeed, pre-Bach-like), much less preoccupied with the expressive possibilities of the large organ. Perhaps Hindemith, with all his dissonances, and Howells, with all his archaisms, are two of the last of the real romantics. But the third period is undoubtedly with us in the work of Messiaen, who for the first time treats the organ as a precision instrument of science.[3] While we have romantic organs we shall continue to play, and demand, music that suits them. Baroque-style organs will demand the baroque of the Continental reformed and liturgy-conscious organists. The organ is no better than the piano for the expression of true serial music, although some has found its way into the literature. But Messiaen, the end product of the process begun by Debussy, combines a sure contact with romantic values with a quite new approach to the instrument, and in this is clearly the man of the new age.

The piano and the romantic organ between them have, however, conditioned the musical appreciation of the churchgoer, to whom Messiaen would be a scandal, and Pepping a dry pedant. The conditioning continues. What we have now to ask is, who were the people behind this fashion? The piano, and the appreciation of the special qualities of the romantic organ (and conversely, the dislike and suspicion of chamber music, the harpsichord, unaccompanied vocal music, and baroque organs) go with a way of life, and their association with that way of life is as unquestionably historical as any such connection can ever be judged to be.

The Pianists

Who were they? Let us remind ourselves of the salient points in Loesser's analysis.

[3] See *Twentieth Century Church Music*, pp. 130-33.

1. They believed mystically in "liberty."

2. They believed in unrestrained expression in word and tone, and in the emphatic utterance of humane sentiment.

3. They believed in the right of all human beings to the opportunity for self-development.

4. They believed in money and in the palpable evidences of its assured possession.

5. They believed that woman's place is in the home.

6. They spun dreams about heroes and were much given to hero worship.

7. They cultivated virtuosos whose feats commanded the attention of thousands.

Among the Christian churches familiar to us, whom does all this suggest? Not the Anglican church reformed by the Oxford Movement (nor, come to that, the Anglican church unreformed by it); the ideals there were the discipline of liturgy and the primarily rustic virtues of the surviving feudal society. Certainly not the newly revived monastic orders. Not the emancipated Roman Catholics. Not the social missionaries of Moody and Sankey or General Booth. No. Irresistibly this character sketch suggests the liberal Protestant: the Congregationalist or Baptist in England, the Free Church Scotsman of 1900, the Eastern seaboard American Protestant.

Is not this right? Do not Reformed Christians believe in "liberty"; is not that why, as we claim, we are not Catholics or Episcopalians? Do not we enthrone the preacher in our services, and did not we, before we lost our nerve, foster, encourage, and delight in the dramatic rhetoric of the pulpit (the "unrestrained expression" of high sentiment, the cult of the virtuoso of the City Temple or Riverside Church, New York)? Were we not given to hero worship directed toward our great preachers? Did we not lead the thought of three generations in promoting humanitarian ideas and pleading for the rights of man? Were we not an essentially masculine culture in our great days—did we not see more responsible men in our congregations than any other church culture did? And (need we be altogether ashamed of it?) did we not believe in money? Did we not make a considerable liturgical exercise of the collection in church, lay public emphasis on the need for stewardship, advertise our collections in monthly newsletters, and erect buildings which spoke, some eloquently, some stridently, some with bestial vulgarity, of the expense that had gone into their making?

One of the points which there has not been time to make within the scope of this chapter is that the culture I have been speaking of, the culture of the piano, of romanticism, is an urban culture. It is quite misunderstood if it is thought of as a rustic culture. But it is firmly and undivorcibly wedded to liberal Protestantism. It is losing its nerve just at the moment when it needs to regain it. Professor Harvey Cox's book, *The Secular City*, challenges us to believe in this inheritance and not to repudiate it. So I am not repudiating it here. I am only illustrating it, drawing it to my readers' attention, and pleading that we do not allow it to become paralyzed.

If we are not aware of how what we stand for came about, we shall not be aware of the origin of our present problems. The need which history presses on us is for a genuine urban culture, not (this was the limitation of romanticism) for an urban culture administered by people who really wanted to go and live in villages as soon as they could afford to. The whole contention of my argument is that a church music is waiting to be born that is relevant to the culture which the romantics half-admitted and which it is our generation's business wholly to admit. What the piano devotee did not reckon with in the days when pianos

sold by the scores of thousands is that the city which provided the money spent on the piano contained slums. For
our romantic and humanitarian grandfathers the city was
the successful. The failures were left to Moody and Sankey.
Now their grandchildren are playing guitars.

6. alien forms of music

The Insular Music-Lover

The church is now being confronted by many forms of music which seem alien to its long-standing traditions. There are advocates of jazz, of "pop" music, of electronic music, of twelve-tone music, and there is no telling what the next suggestion may be. In all such cases controversy of a kind follows on the question whether these alien forms are legitimate.

Now the argument of the preceding chapter was designed to make the point that churchmen's reactions to alien forms of music are often conditioned by social forces which are insufficiently recognized for what they are. We arrived at the provisional conclusion that at least it is easy to see why the musical taste of the average Protestant congregation in Britain or America is so limited. We also found that the "music-lover's" standards of criticism are unreliable in judging church music. Had we taken the time and space to deal with the traditional church music of other accessible cultures, such as that of Wales or of Gaelic-speaking Scotland, we should have seen how people who are innocent of the culture of the "music-lover" can keep alive a very robust, although inevitably localized,

108

tradition of religious music. The hymn tunes of Wales and
the incantations of Gaelic Scotland are precisely not the
products of men who went to concerts, listened to broad-
casts, and moved in cosmopolitan circles of musical culture.
That is why the Welsh miner has, or until recently had,
a repertory of hymns which he knew by heart and would
sing in any kind of circumstances where more than two or
three were gathered together; beside that repertory the
English working man's knowledge of any kind of music
has always been minimal. The only Welshmen who write
string quartets and symphonies are Welshmen who have
caught on to European culture.

And what we want to drive home is this point: that
despite the freedom with which he moves in a culture
of a whole continent, the "music-lover" can turn out to be
just as provincial, just as much socially conditioned, just
as narrow and exclusive in his musical judgments and ap-
prehensions as he would judge the Welsh miner to be.

When we talk of alien music nowadays in reasonably cultivated church circles we mean jazz, pop, electronics, and
twelve-tone. But to the conservative cathedral canon the
music of William Byrd is alien music; to the ordinary
church musician of 1890 (let alone the musically uncul-
tivated member of the congregation) practically anything
written earlier than 1800 was alien music. I can personally
remember one of the earliest performances in England of
Fauré's *Requiem* (in Oxford under John Webster, in 1941),
when that work, composed in 1887, the same year as
Stainer's *Crucifixion*, sounded quite remarkably alien. (It
may be added that now, 25 years later, it is among the
works most regularly performed by reputable church choirs
—and rightly so.) In the days when Alfred Hollins
flourished, and among the people for whom he worked,
anything but nineteenth-century Germanic music was alien.

More About Jazz

We must therefore recognize that judgments of jazz music, based, however unconsciously and unintendedly, on the ground that it is alien, that the church is not used to it, that it is incongruous with the church's customs of thought, have at best a very limited value. If it is alien, the fact can be noted—but so must other facts.

One of these is that (as we have said) jazz has an authentically religious root in the spiritual of the American Negro. Another is that it is now a serious and sophisticated musical form. A third is that the confrontation of the church as we know it with the issue of jazz music is the inevitable outcome of the new anthropological dispensation which has brought about the sharing of territories by different races and the confrontation of one race by the demands and values of another. These are historical facts which simply have to be noted and accepted.

Now the reasons given by the modern puritan (and he is the "music-lover" par excellence, the piano-centered man, the admirer of hard work and lover of virtuosity) for resisting jazz are social. If the puritan-romantic admires discipline, he is made uncomfortable by the demonstrativeness of jazz and by its tradition and practice of ecstatic improvisation. If he admires hard work he suspects the jazz musician of being able to do things too easily. And if, as he certainly will be, he is much more at home with intellectual activity (which he may well call "spiritual") than with the crudities of the human body, which his scientific culture has done so much to remove from his sight, then the physical affinities of jazz will offend him. Moreover, not to put too fine a point on it, the puritan is a patriot, at heart even a jingo, and jazz is, as the self-expression of a subject race, an embarrassment to him.

None of these judgments is musical—not even the ones which can be expressed in musical terms. They are all social. And the interesting thing is that they can be heard quite frequently from people who in their worship have traditionally extolled the practices of ecstatic preaching and free prayer. The only thing to do with a puritan who insists on stopping at social judgments of jazz is to persuade him how much of a jazzman he himself is in his own way.

There is something aggressive and candid about jazz which makes other kinds of people hesitant to allow it in the church. There are many who still feel that the proper relation between the church and the musician is that of master and servant; whose characteristic comment on any sign of invention or initiative in an organist is that he was "enjoying himself" (a rather sinister way to behave in church). This outlook is happiest when the musician is subject strictly to a text; it requires what we earlier called fundamentalism in the musician. And although, as we also saw, it is demonstrably impossible for the church musician to show this literal musical obedience in his day-to-day work, what usually happens is a tolerable accommodation in which the musician sees that what he does do creatively is noticed—if by anyone—only by the sympathetic.

What is remarkable is that rational Protestants (and for all I know, rational Catholics as well) have so rarely argued from the real nature of jazz. The real story is infinitely more alarming than is usually admitted. The churchman's case against jazz is at the same time weaker and stronger than he usually realizes.

The Case for and Against Jazz

On the one hand, jazz has this religious origin. That origin is inseparable from quite unbelievable human suffering. The suffering out of which the "spiritual" came is a byword of history; everybody who knows any history knows that. Everybody agrees that slavery in the form it took when Wilberforce aroused the British nation against it, and when not much later the Civil War flared up in America, is an abomination. The spirituals come from a time when dogma was irrelevant, from men who had no past that they could bear to remember, and no present that might not be defaced with degradation and terror, and no worldly future that they could dare to contemplate. Their subject was not the doctrine but the folklore of Christianity —Christ's redemption and the promise of heaven. They were saturated with apocalyptic prophecy.

Jazz has in one sense come far from that. But in all its stages jazz has been no less topical, fantastic, and intimate than the spirituals were. By all accounts, when jazz first crossed the frontier between the sacred and the secular, it was much more a folk cult than a commercial empire. It was never thought by the unnamed and unhonored jazz musicians of the earliest days that jazz would become the idol that it now is. It is most significant, for example, that at a very early stage in its emergence as a popular cult in America, it found its home in the rent parties that were organized in the days of Prohibition.[1]

It was, like the folk song movement of the sixties, essentially an "underground" cult, an in-group activity. It was as much, and for the same reasons, an in-group activity as the singing of hymns is among Christians. Negro migration from the south, the availability of records, and the attraction of the esoteric all combined to make jazz a nationwide cult within a decade (the twenties), but it was these inevitable accidents rather than any innate property of the jazz form that made the New Orleans kings famous. And

[1] See Lillian Erlich, *What Jazz Is All About* (New York: Julian Messner, 1962), chap. 8.

like contemporary folk music (or anybody's folk music), jazz was associated with the basic things, the basic hopes and protests, of humanity. There is nothing here, apart from the emphasis on *eros*, to shock the puritan. (He has to pull up in his tracks whenever *eros* rears its ugly head—this always was his main problem.) And even when jazz becomes (as it has become) a public demonstration, what is there in this to shock the churchman who regards the public confession of sin, the public adoration of a crucified Redeemer, as a normal part of his life? It may be terrifying to see people as naked as the jazz singer or player makes himself emotionally when he goes into his traditional routines; but is this ecstasy and emotion any more remarkable than that for which some of our hymns, and many of their tunes, ask us?

In these ways the case against jazz is weak. Where its advocate runs into rough water is when its social accompaniments come into the picture. It is impossible to be unaware that jazz playing has at present a tragically close connection with the worst of modern carnal corruptions. One can understand the difficulty which an ordinary Christian finds in having to do with any cult in which there is so much sexual license and drug traffic. Can an art be authentic when it seems to have such grievous associations?

Of one of the greatest figures of modern jazz, one commentator writes:

[He] is the great tragic hero of jazz. He led, by ordinary standards, a miserable life. Hooked on narcotics at the age of fifteen, he spent most of his life, as he said himself, "on a panic." . . . His money went to narcotics peddlers, so that no matter how much he earned, he seldom had good clothes or a decent place to live.[2]

[2] *Ibid.*, pp. 146, 150.

This musician, we are told, having had four marriages, died at thirty-five after a final five years "beset by illnesses and emotional storms." The story can be paralleled too often in the jazz and pop world, say the critics, to be healthy.

A puritan resistance to all this is perfectly understandable. An attitude such as that taken up on Charles Cleall's book, *Music and Holiness*,[3] that the Christian worshiper should be sheltered from all contact with the scandals of the world, is to a large extent logical and accepted by many. But just as we are on the point of saying, "No! we really draw the line at drugs," we remember that the fathers of the primitive church were exceedingly worried at the thought of any musical instrument being used in church, because of the secular associations which their sound would recall. We remember that the Scots Kirk would not allow organs in church until the nineteenth century was well advanced. (The first organ in a parish church in Scotland was installed in 1865.) Let there be no mistake: the opponents of instruments in churches were concerned not with excluding the world from the church's concern but with excluding vice and corruption from the church's customs.

It may also be recalled that people who appreciate the music of Wagner are untroubled by what is reported of his personal morals. But the whole issue is really subtler than this. What has to be decided is whether the stressful, tragic, ecstatic world of jazz is or is not intimately and inextricably bound to a habit of vice and false religion. Must we, or how long must we, play Michal to David's dance? What are Christians to make of a passage like this:

[Gregorian chant] at first was but a simple modal form in which certain religious people could express the ardour of their

---

[3] London: Epworth Press, 1964.

hearts and souls. And it still remains that today. . . . It lives on, perpetuated by the few as one of the most purely expressive and evocative of musical forms. For quiet grandeur it has almost never been approached.

Notice that I say *almost* never . . . for the Gregorian chant has a close brother—no, not in the classical music which developed over and around it, not even in the liturgical music which followed closely in its path, but in the *blues!* Yes, the blues are the blood brother of the early religious chant. It fulfilled the same purpose—gave the singer a complete emotional release through a specific technique: to cleanse oneself in the eyes of God through a deeply religious experience. The form of the chant and the blues is similar—the purpose similar. In the history of music they occupy similar roles and are inherently closer to each other than to any other music.[4]

Plenty of Christians would comment that the author of this outburst is taking too much on himself in assuming that the experiences associated with plainsong and with the blues are in the same sense religious. And yet, when one recalls the contention of Fr. G. B. Chambers[5] that the genius of plainsong is far from being the austere and bloodless thing that some interpreters have made it, but is rather of the ecstatic and prophetic kind, one pauses. Nonetheless, the impressive answer of the conservative evangelicals, as expressed by Charles Cleall deserves to be noticed: "Harman and Mellers tell us (in *Man and His Music*) that jazz 'tends to encourage a state of trance.' In the phrase used by our adolescents, 'it sends you.' Where does it send you?" [6]

So the argument goes on. In my own view it cannot be

[4] J. Wood, "Reflections on the Nature of Jazz," in *Jazzbook*, A. J. McCarthy, ed. (London: Cassell & Company, 1955), p. 120.
[5] In *Folksong-Plainsong: Study in Musical Origins* (London: Merlin Press, 1956).
[6] *Music and Holiness*, p. 59.

settled dogmatically. When all is said, music is music, and not semantics or morals. But practical decisions are normally moral decisions. All that I can hope to achieve in this argument is to point to the fact that it is not legitimate either to say that jazz music is always good in church or to say that nineteenth-century romantic music is always good in church. The exclusive preference of one style is no better than the exclusive preference of another. There is little doubt that an exclusive diet of Stainer and Barnby "induces a state of trance." There is never any need, in a Christian context, to "write off" any whole class of music, either Dunstable or Palestrina, Stockhausen or Count Basie, Schönberg or John Stainer—for any reason other than one of these—by saying that it is demonstrably bad music, or that it is demonstrably imprudent to use it in *this* situation.

The Cult of Pop

When we turn to "pop" music, our chief difficulty is that it is exceedingly difficult to define. Jazz can be defined with some precision, pop cannot. Pop is that which appeals to the masses of people in modern Western urban civilizations. Its appeal is shown by its sales on cheap record discs and in sheet music form.

We all know what we mean nowadays by "pop." But one has only to hear a small selection of pop tunes to realize that to categorize anything as "pop" is to make a judgment that is entirely social, and not musical at all. Perhaps it is not too hazardous to say that the normal pop tune—that which, in the language of the cult, "makes the charts" in any particular week—is basically a very simple tune, not far removed in its simplicity from a hymn tune. Indeed, it is only a crass lack of ingenuity and observation (which I have no intention of enlightening here)

that has preserved the church from a large-scale importa-
tion of current pop tunes as hymns. Many more of them
would make hymns than those which have actually been
used as such.[7] But there was the celebrated case of the tune
composed for Christian words in a German Evangelical
Academy which Miss Petula Clark made into a chart hitter
called "Thank You" (and a very good tune it is, too).
Technically, a tune becomes "pop" when it has been
noticed by a large enough group of people.

The truth perhaps is that it is production that makes a
pop tune into a three-day legend. The adjudicators in
"Juke Box Jury" judge a pop tune on a single hearing,
and it stands or falls by an immediate impression. There
is no musical definition that covers all pop tunes; they are
very evidently made, not born. In themselves they may
be musically interesting, or musically tedious. Everything
depends on how they are presented, and on the whim of
mass opinion.

So it is really very difficult to get hold of any principle
by which one can judge the usefulness of this sort of music
in church. Basically the problem is too simple to need more
than a moment's discussion. Most pop tunes are in themselves so uninteresting as to offer no competition even to
second-rate church music, and there is simply nothing to
be gained by importing them into the church as tunes.
Whether one wants to import into the church the separable
accidents that make pop tunes what they are is another
question.

If it is true that pop music is not primarily music, but
a way of life, then we have a real problem on our hands:
more acute than that of jazz, because jazz really is music—

---

[7] Such as, for example, "Michael, row the boat ashore," which is sung
to hymns in the meter 7.7.7.7. It is about as interesting as the English
tune to "Rock of Ages."

it is musically definable. I myself suspect that while jazz
has a possible place in Christian worship, pop has, strictly
speaking, none whatever. I fancy that the objections to pop
are the same as the objections to an exclusive diet of
Stainer.

For what in practice makes pop different from other
kinds of music? The answer must be (1) prodigious commercial publicity, (2) the worship of pop virtuosos, with all
its attendant juvenile mystique, and (3) the habit of producing and enduring a quite extravagant amount of noise.
If one believes in introducing this style to church worship,
one must imply a belief in these three attendant principles.
Modern evangelism of a certain kind does believe in them
to a certain extent—in saturation publicity, in the mystique
surrounding a glamorous preacher, and in the producing,
not precisely of an enormous and oppressive noise, but of
an impression of overwhelming power and competence
through the big uniformed, regimented choir. It is impossible to think that the music of the Beatles is really
out of place in a crusaders' tent; the crusaders would probably disapprove of the Beatles more because they are com-
petitors than because they are a principle of evil.

I refrain from judgment; I merely point out that the
evangelistic techniques of some contemporary crusaders are
pop techniques: essentially undistinguished music is "produced" with bands, electronic organs, large choirs, and
soloists, so as to sound impressive. With a mere twist of
technique it would not be difficult to convert the decorous
walk to the platform of the converts into the screaming
surge of Beatle-worshipers toward the stage. But without
any abstract moralizing it can be said that where the presuppositions of any Christian community include the com-
mendation of rationality, self-restraint and the worship
not of human beings but of God, the pop technique is in-

congruous. Unless the inducing of some kind of trance in the worshiper is the avowed aim of the worship, the intense rhythmic noise of pop will defeat rational worship. The quotation from Charles Cleall which we cited just now continues thus:

Dr. Ian Oswald, Beit Memorial Research Fellow at the Institute of Experimental Psychology at the University of Oxford,[8] wrote in 1958 of his experiments there, "Loud, rhythmic noise helps people to escape from reality into a dream-world where they no longer have to be awake. Because of the tendency to breathe in time to the music, people can breathe too fast and too hard. Overbreathing greatly reduces the blood-flow to the brain, and can seriously impair a person's consciousness." [9]

There need be little doubt among laymen of the medical truth that exposure to excessive noise is psychologically and physically harmful, and therefore that the extravagant amplification of sound through guitar amplifiers is a dangerous and deplorable practice.

The Case Against Pop

Sociologists have argued that the cult of noise has provided an outlet for elemental tendencies in young people which can produce more antisocial effects if otherwise directed. It was said at the time when the "Mersey beat" cult was appearing in Liverpool (the home of the Beatles) that a marked decline in juvenile delinquency and vandalism coincided with its appearance. The complexity of the world of pop may further be judged from the following extract from an article celebrating a more recently formed

[8] At the time of the book's publication, and at the time of the present writing, Dr. Oswald is attached to the research staff of Edinburgh University and Edinburgh Royal Infirmary.

[9] *Music and Holiness*, p. 59.

group of singers, inscrutably called "The Who." The article quotes Chris Stamp and Martin Lambert, joint managers of this group:

> To my mind, their act creates emotions of anger and violence, and a thousand other things I don't really understand myself. . . . Their rootlessness appeals to the kids. They're really a new form of crime—armed against the bourgeois. The point is, we're not saying, Here are four nice, clean-cut lads come to entertain you. We're saying, Here is something outrageous—go wild! [10]

That which corresponds in pop to the drugs that defile the jazz world is undoubtedly the appalling cynicism and patronage of the pop establishment. If we set aside the drugs from jazz, somehow we must distinguish pop from its unlovely surroundings. But even so, there is an artificiality about the pop world which seems to go to its very heart.

For pop is not so much a musical form as a gesture. My case here indeed is simply that jazz is a musical form, while pop is not. If drug-taking were inseparable from the essence of jazz, then jazz would be incompatible with any Christian activity. But the striking of attitudes, the counterfeiting of violence, the blowing off of rebellious stream that seem to characterize pop have no place at all in the conduct of the church. The fact that a tune is popular does not make it incompatible with worship. But the associations of pop are largely contradictory of worship, and I am arguing that without them pop would not be pop.

The words of pop songs may come from anywhere, like the tunes. They may be Negro spirituals like "Michael, row the boat ashore," or they may be, like those of jazz, about the basic intimacies of human life, principally eros.

[10] The Observer, Colour Supplement, March 20, 1966.

Occasionally they are yearning and quasi-mystical. Very rarely do they have any distinction that Christian hymns do not improve on. In the pop culture they matter very little. An English headmaster, Donald Hughes of Rydal school, was speaking to a conference of the Hymn Society in 1965 about hymns, and he made the following interesting comparison between the approach of most people to the words of hymns and that of the young toward their culture songs. Having just noted how many people disregard altogether the words of hymns, he went on:

This is something to which the modern generation is very accustomed. In the world of popular music the words often hardly bear examination. The best of them spring from a folklore which is quite remote from contemporary life. The obvious example is the mythology of Negro spirituals. A few years ago the Black and White Minstrels made very popular a song which repeated the line, "Michael, row the boat ashore." I once asked a sixth form who Michael was and what he was doing in a boat. None of them knew and none of them thought it mattered. . . .

One of the inept things which Adam Faith said in his television discussion with the Archbishop of York was that the church was at fault in its hymns, because the lyrics were incomprehensible. My point is that a great many popular songs are rooted in a mythology which people no longer understand, but that this doesn't stop them singing them.[11]

Perhaps we may add that nearly all the products of composers who have sought to integrate pop idioms with the needs of church music arouse the principal complaint

[11] Donald Hughes, "Hymns in School Worship," in the *Bulletin of the Hymn Society of Great Britain & Ireland*, No. 104, September, 1965, p. 31. Adam Faith, a formerly celebrated pop singer, met the Archbishop of York in a much-publicized television interview in 1962, having challenged the Archbishop to a debate after a statement by the Archbishop in a diocesan newspaper to the effect that Adam Faith's songs were obsessed with sex.

that musically they are exceedingly dull, and that it is difficult to see in what sense the pop hymn tunes of the Twentieth-Century Church Light Music Group in England are better than those they are meant to replace. Malcolm Williamson's pop hymn tunes are sometimes very good tunes, sometimes terrible ones which deceive the listener only when production pulls the wool over his ears. If any confirmation is needed of the very obvious point made earlier that there is no such thing as a pop style in music, the astonishing diversity of style in Williamson's tunes (I think the best description of them is "vernacular" tunes) provides it.[12] The absence so far (since the inception of the style by Geoffrey Beaumont in 1956) of the emergence of any recognizably authentic "popular" style in hymn tunes suggests that it is a complex of customs and a set of values rather than a musical style which the advocates of this kind of music are commending.

But there are certain adjuncts of the pop style which are certainly not self-evidently incongruous with Christian worship, the chief of which is the use of the guitar. This, played properly and unadulterated by amplifiers, is an instrument of great beauty. It is unsuitable, because of its gentle sound, for the accompaniment of massed singing, and it is not, like some traditional instruments, effective when multiplied. But what it can do is accompany the solo voice, and most effectively in carols or folk songs.

Folk Song

The recent revival of folk singing is a notable social development in Britain and America, and this again has had

---

[12] See the three books, each containing thirty "20th Century Hymns," and *12 Hymn Tunes*, by Malcolm Williamson, together with certain observations on this matter in *Twentieth Century Church Music*.

some impact on the church, chiefly in Britain through the work of Sydney Carter.[13] In many ways this is an alien form to most churchgoers; principally because folk songs need to be sung by soloists, ideally accompanying themselves on a guitar, and sometimes, but not always, provide a refrain in which the whole company can join.

Now the folk song movement (which in its earlier forms we have mentioned already) has led people to think of folk songs as demure and rustic pieces printed, with suitable omissions in the words, in specialist journals. Most people know that a few current hymn tunes are arrangements, usually by Vaughan Williams, of English folk songs going back to the early ages of England's music-making. It has to be remembered that folk songs were quite often work songs, like sea shanties, and that if they are rustic in their words, this is because in the time of their creation England was rustic culture. The modern folk song is most often a protest song, a song of anger and purposefulness. For this there are many respectable precedents of which the most familiar is the eighteenth-century version of the British National Anthem, with its violent second verse

> Confound their politics
> Frustrate their knavish tricks,
> On thee our hopes we fix,
>   God save us all!

But most protest movements of the post-Revolutionary days had their folk songs—Ebenezer Elliott's Chartist hymn comes near to the folk-song style:

[13] I have referred to this both in *Twentieth Century Church Music* and in *Hymns Today and Tomorrow* (Nashville: Abingdon Press, 1964). See also *9 Carols or Ballads* (London: Clarion Press, 1963) and *10 New Songs* (Clarion Press, 1965), both by Sydney Carter.

When wilt thou save the people,
O God of mercy, when?

The modern folk song spends much of its time protesting against religion, as part of a general protest against the
established order of things. It is well known that in the
folk-song "underground" in Britain there are plenty of
young Communists, even anarchists; what is not always
so widely canvassed is that there are plenty of young
Catholics in it as well. In words I personally heard from
Sydney Carter himself, "They argue about each other's
beliefs and borrow each other's guitars."

The fact that atheist anarchism and Communism are
prominent among the folk singers makes the church un-
derstandably cautious about their techniques. Moreover,
folk singing is rapidly becoming a commercial cult like
pop, and its underground culture does share some of the
less lovely attributes of the jazz culture.

The great thing, however, is that in Britain the church
noticed Sydney Carter before most of its members became
aware of the disagreeable associations of folk song in the
way that they became aware of those of jazz or pop. So
in fact there is not as yet (at least in Britain) any violent
reaction against it. It is perfectly easy to present a Christian folk singer in a Scottish church where it would still
be hazardous to present jazz, or, if one believed in it, pop.
What is more, there are attempts currently to harness the
folk-song style for Christian purposes, inspired by Carter.[14]

The distinction of folk song is that the words matter,
in a sense in which in jazz and pop they do not matter.
The tune is usually simple, commonplace, but innocently

[14] See, for example, No. 9 in the experimental leaflet, *Dunblane Praises*
(Dunblane: Scottish Churches' House, 1964), and certain examples in
Sing! (Edinburgh, 1965).

sound. It may be an old tune, or an old tune with a few elementary alterations. The new folk song may even be a revival, in the style of Joan Baez, of an old song with its tune. But what folk songs can do—as jazz and pop at present cannot—is reflect faithfully and precisely the prevailing mood of a culture. They can express the world's unregenerate needs, often through irony and anger; they can say things, sung by a soloist, that hymns cannot, communally sung, begin to say. It is in respect of folk song alone of these three alien forms that I myself am prepared to say, "If public worship as we know it cannot accommodate this, then we ought to consider altering public worship so that it can."

But this has led us to the threshold of our next chapter.

IV
the dimension
of drama

7. worship and the anglicans

Worship Is Drama

The truth which needs to be emphasized in Protestant circles above all others, when Christian worship is under discussion, is that worship is essentially drama. Catholics have never really forgotten this, and there are vestiges of its recall in the worship of Anglicans. Historical reasons have conspired to cause Protestants to dismiss it from their consciousness altogether; and like anything else which is dismissed from consciousness, the truth has erupted in places where it has been beyond the range of conscious criticism. It therefore still shocks the Protestant to be told that his central demand is that his preacher shall be an artist; he is surprised to learn[1] that the Reformed churches have excelled in one branch of art—that of rhetoric; and he is pained when people outside his tradition compare his adulation of the great Victorian preachers as made of the same stuff as the contemporary adulation of film stars and pop singers.

But worship is drama. It cannot be anything else. It is

[1] For example, from Caryl Micklem in his contribution to *Church and the Visual Arts*, ed., Gilbert Cope (London: Faith Press, 1964).

corporate *action*. It is equally important to point out that it is not what people often think of as drama—and in doing this we are doing exactly what we have just been doing with church music. "Drama" to so many people has a connotation just as narrow as that which we have been saying has damaged the image of church music.

To be specific: what we do not here mean is that worship is an entertainment put on at one end of a building for the amusement of people at the other end. We do not wish to compare worship with the plays of St. John Ervine, even if it might be not entirely absurd to compare liberal Protestant worship with the plays of Bernard Shaw. What we mean is rather that worship is what we are coming in our own time, largely by the revival of ancient techniques, to see to be drama. Just as the revival of the music of the English Tudors, the continental polyphonists, Purcell, and Schütz has not only enriched the repertory but made possible an altogether larger and deeper view of what church music is, so the new interest in the apron stage, or "theater-in-the-round," the revival of medieval mysteries and moralities, and the swing away from plot-centered drama (as from tune-centered music) has opened up the possibility of seeing a truth about worship and drama which has long been hidden from large sections of the church.

If you say that drama is designed to amuse an audience, you speak too narrowly. It is better to say that drama is an action performed by people set aside to do it, and designed to involve an audience. The involvement may be emotional or mental; it may indeed be the involvement of amusement; but it may well be more than any of these. The revolt of our own dramatists against all the things that separate the actors from the audience, that make for fantasy or unreality in drama, is familiar enough. The apron stage brings the actors out among the audience (where they were in Shakespeare's time); theater-in-the-round makes it necessary for the audience to see actors in all their dimensions, not only from the front (as they did in the days of the Athenian dramatists). The suggestive use of levels and conventional symbols, the absence of specific scenery, bring the audience's imagination into play by substituting suggestion for statement.

Audience Participation

Audience participation naturally follows. First there are primitive experiments in making the audience appear to take part in the play. In Eliot's *Murder in the Cathedral*, the sermon is the first shock, and the addresses of the three murderers are the second and greater; in the commentator-intermediary, who in the occasional nineteenth-century farce, or in Thornton Wilder's *Our Town*, addresses the audience while the action is proceeding we have an allied technique. There is Benjamin Britten's *Let's Make an Opera* in which the rehearsal of the audience is part of the "action," and leads to direct audience participation in the short opera, when it comes to be formally acted as the second half of the show. And then there are the intimate revues, such as that incomparable show, *The Second City*, in which for the second half of the evening's entertainment the audience suggested subjects on which the performers improvised sketches. There was Hans-Rudi Weber's experiment at a conference associated with the German *Kirchentag* which originated the idea of "socio-drama"— the improvising of a sketch or charade which would show in action some moral problem which in verbal discussion had defeated the participants.

As soon as one lets one's mind play around such notions as these—and all the parallels one could think of—one is reminded of the experiments that are taking place in church building today, where the center of operations in worship is being moved from the far end of a long building to the middle of a square one—precisely the application of "theatre-in-the-round" to worship. We recall that among Roman Catholics, who have never lost their sense of the drama of the Eucharist, the great need of bringing back congregational participation in it has now been answered in local custom and in the developments of the Second Vatican Council.

Illustration from Coventry

What I propose here to show is that while there is no question that public worship is drama, there are bound to be differences of view on whether it is as it were "scripted" drama or "domestic" drama. I can make this distinction clearer when we have considered certain examples in current practice, and extracted their dramatic content. But the alignment of the true controversy—not whether worship is drama but what kind of drama it is— can be well illustrated by reference to the celebrated story of the building of Coventry Cathedral, as Sir Basil Spence records it in his book, *Phoenix at Coventry*.[2]

Basil Spence's first sketches of his design (which in the end turn out to be very like the finished product) were submitted and adjudged the winners of the competition in August, 1951. Only a month or two later, the architect was asked to meet the Bishop of Coventry (then Dr. Neville Gorton). Spence's plan had placed the altar far back, right at the "east" end of the cathedral, but in full sight of all the congregation. The bishop suggested that the altar should be moved right forward—not to a central position, but to the west end of the chancel so that it would be physically as near the front of the congregation

[2] (London: Geoffrey Bles, 1964.)

as it could be brought. The architect was completely won over. Indeed, he had seen this style in many continental churches. In the end the revised plan, supported by the bishop and the architect, was thrown out uncompromisingly by the Reconstruction Committee and the altar does now stand very near the far east wall, under the great tapestry.

The interesting point for us is how the Bishop saw this scheme.

The Bishop talked in a wonderful way about the gathering of the flock, saying that they could kneel anywhere on the three altar steps and that the Sacrament should be given individually to each. . . . We discussed the function and position of the choir. . . . But the Bishop was impatient with this point of view, as he asserted that the Sacrament of Communion was the important thing, and singing quite secondary. . . .

This was the plan on which we finally decided. The altar was brought right forward with only three steps up from the nave, so that the Holy Table itself could be strong, big and simple. Immediately behind would be the choir and somehow an organ console would have to be fitted in; and beyond that the Clergy-stalls in a "U" shape, with the Bishop's throne in the center on the axis.

Dr. Gorton [the Bishop] fidgeted and said, "I don't want to be in the center." [3]

It could not be clearer that the late Bishop of Coventry saw the Sacrament of Communion as central to the worship of the church, and as a family occasion. Instead of the formality of the Anglican "Communion rail" (which he would retain only marginally to the architecture, because it was a physical convenience for old people), he saw his congregation kneeling "anywhere on the three steps"; the musical appointments, the ceremonious implications of the Eucharist, did not interest him at all.

[3] *Ibid.*, pp. 42-43.

Domestic or Ceremonious?

When the opening of the Cathedral came, on May 25, 1962, the good Bishop Gorton had died, and a new bishop reigned. The consecration service was one of the most perfect and well-proportioned pieces of "production drama" that the Church of England has conceived in our time. It was on a level with the Coronation service of 1953—but in one way more powerful because of its magnificently revised and retranslated liturgical diction, and because of the sense of purposeful, almost pugnacious resolution which the new bishop, in his personal approach to the massive part which he had to play in the service, lent to the whole occasion. Dr. Bardsley, the new (and present) bishop, has been criticized for "theatricality"—a criticism which could not have been offered without complete absurdity to his predecessor. He is one of the most forceful and effective preachers in the Church of England. From the beginning to the end of that service it was quite clear that he saw the occasion as a drama, and as production drama, not domestic drama. This might well be a Christian family, but it was also the symbolic people of God. The manner, as it turned out, matched the matter. The cathedral in its completed form is a production theater, relying on distance, movement, and ceremony for the effect of what it says in its worship, as the European cathedrals always have done. And although many criticisms have been made of the completed work, there may be this to be said for the style which was, against Bishop Gorton's wishes, adopted: that if you really wanted a family drama, if you wanted to play down the "trajectory" notion of worship drama, then it would really have been necessary to alter the whole shape of the building. Given that traditionally long, narrow site, it was probably right to pursue the implications of *length* to their natural conclusion; and in terms of dramatic values there is no choice between an intimate altar and an altar to and from which there is a longish walk. Both "say" something perfectly valid about the relation of worship to life.

There is so much, indeed, that architecture can say that it is always unwise to become wedded to any single school of thought without considering local practicalities. The "mystery" of the medieval cathedral which shut off the altar altogether from the common worshiper's sight is a perfectly valid point to make, even if somehow it needs supplementing by something else (like the medieval rood screen) which proclaims the nearness of the gospel to the world. The great chapel at Kelham (Nottinghamshire)[4] hides its altar in darkness at the time of the Eucharist: in the early morning the worshiper walks under the great cross erected on the rood arch to the altar, behind which there is no east window; he walks back into a splash of light directed into the center of the floor by a window in the roof. At Coventry the altar is at the geographical north, and light is directed toward it from the angled windows in the east wall. The worshiper sees the many-colored light as he goes to the altar; returning, he sees its source for the first time in the windows which are now visible to him. This is a variation on the same theme. In building churches nowadays architects are using the natural resources of light and ground level in the manner in which the artists of the medieval cathedrals used them; you cannot say everything at once—it is sufficient if what is said is clearly seen to be valid, to correspond with the connection the church must always establish between worship and life.

[4] Illustrated on Plate X in A. G. Hebert's *Liturgy and Society* (London: Faber and Faber, 1961).

Music and This Drama

Ideally then, worship needs to harmonize the elements of remoteness and nearness, the ideas of the family and of the symbolic people of God; and this can be done only by choosing the emphases, and harnessing the natural qualities, that are appropriate to each individual place. But what is always true is that to lose sight of the dramatic factor in worship is to lose altogether the key to making worship practical as well as beautiful.

Church music is part of the drama of worship, and the question for us is what part we can expect it to play in the developments of the drama of worship which we are now witnessing. Church music is at the same time the most powerful generator of a sense of remoteness and scale, and also the most useful medium for congregational participation, being both rhythmical and rational. We are not saying that worship ought to be drama. We are saying that it inescapably is drama. This is the best answer to anybody who accuses musical worship of being a concert or performed sermon-centered worship of being a lecture, or sacramental worship of being a superstitious mummery.

We will now look at four examples of worship activity, and extract from them their content of drama.

Evensong as Programming

Evening prayer in the Book of Common Prayer of the Church of England is a scripted drama of venerable history. Its dramatic content can be assessed under four heads.

1. Historical

Evening prayer is, in its origin, an "office," not an evangelical service. It was compiled from medieval services that were designed to be said or sung within religious communities. The technique of worship in these communities is something which the modern layman knows little about. The assumption is that there will be a number of people, small (as in a mountain community in medieval Wales) or very large (as in medieval France), all living in one building or block of buildings at whose center there is a place of worship. All are engaged in aspects of the same work—study, contemplation, scholarship, cooking, sweeping, gardening, trading, and serving the poor. That is a typical medieval monastery or convent. The day's work is punctuated, for all ranks, by *short* periods of worship together in the communal chapel—which in a large abbey will be known as the abbey church, and will be a building of great architectural splendor and sensitiveness. The contemplatives will spend much of the rest of the day in prayer and vigil, but the corridor sweepers and the abbey accountants alike will be involved in the regular periods of worship. Every few hours everybody drops what he is doing and goes to the church. They all know each other well—they all live and work within a few score yards of the church door. In the course of their worship they go through a ritual routine which includes (among many other things) the reading of the psalms once a month, the New Testament twice a year, and the Old Testament (substantially) once a year—those being the activities prescribed for the services out of which morning and evening prayer were formed at the Reformation, and which are continued in those services to this day where they are kept up.

To such a pattern of life a service of worship lasting a quarter of an hour or twenty minutes is appropriate—a detail which is itself strange enough to modern lay people who travel anywhere up to twenty miles on a Sunday to the church of their choice.

Preaching is secondary to community worship of this sort because the community is constantly exercising itself

in prayer, contemplation, reading, and mutual instruction
in the things of the faith. So, although there may be a
sermon at Mass, there is, traditionally, never one at the
Office. The Office is for the people who live in the community; it is the Mass that is for the people who come
in from outside. The shape of the older cathedrals confirms
this: the "choir," separated from the "nave" by a screen,
is the smaller room where the Offices are said or sung; the
"nave" in the larger place where the people from outside
come to hear Mass. When the Office is being said the people round about will hear the abbey bell ring and know that
prayers are being said for them; only for Mass will they
enter the church themselves.

The singing of the Office is then the business of the people in the community; in a large community it is the business of people set aside to do it and is known as the choir.

Anglican evening prayer is an adaptation of this service
to the changed situation in which people are expected to
attend it as an act of *public* worship. From this point of
view it is now widely held that morning and evening prayer
are an unsatisfactory compromise—too rigid, too unadapt-
able to the condition of people who come only occasionally,
too firmly dependent on the historical fact that they are
meant to be daily, not weekly, services. A weekly service
for a scattered congregation is disproportionately short if
it lasts only twenty minutes; so morning and evening prayer
are lengthened by various additions, notably by the addition
of a sermon and of extra prayers and congregational hymns.
These additions are not provided for in the injunctions
which prescribe the order of these services. But they become necessary, because otherwise, if the order is faithfully
followed, the weekly participation of the congregation in
the reading of psalms and scriptures is like reading chapters
on eight, fifteen, and twenty-two of a connected story. It is

not surprising that thoughtful people have reacted against the singing of psalms "in course"—the psalms (with a few well-known exceptions) hardly make sense at all except when read in full and in the context of intensive reading of the rest of Scripture.

Therefore one has to make an imaginative effort to see that evening (or morning) prayer is a drama at all. One sees it best if one attends a sung evensong in an Episcopal cathedral. These services are rightly sung by the choir—the Anglican choir of modern times corresponding to the monks' choir of the Middle Ages. But if one attends evensong in that form, with no sermon and with much sensitive and interpretative singing by the choir, one begins to see what sort of drama it was designed to be.

2. Dialogue

The most obvious sense in which it is a drama is in that it consists of conversation. It provides for conversational prayer, in the form of responses, and for corporate vocal prayer in the saying of certain parts by all present. It provides for a congregational "Amen" as the response to every prayer said by the priest. The buildings appropriate to this sort of worship are constructed so that half the congregation (and half the choir) faces the other half, and the psalms are normally sung antiphonally, that is, "in conversation" by the two halves alternately.

It has to be admitted that the full force of the dialogue in the service of evening prayer is somewhat obscured by accidental difficulties. Not all the responses are in fact in the form of statement and answer; since they are composed of psalm verses divided at the traditional colon between priest and people, the sequence of thought from one half to the other is not normally very clear. One remembers Dean Inge's comment that the Anglican responses sound like a "conversation between two deaf men." The responsive greeting (which comes rather oddly in the middle of evensong)—"the Lord be with you"; "And with thy spirit" —comes a little nearer to recognizable drama. In the form with which the main part of the Coventry consecration opened it is true drama:

The Bishop stands at the west end of the church and greets the people:

In God's name, welcome to you all.

The people reply:

In God's name, welcome to you.

But whatever the limitations of language and technique, the monastic office is *conversation*, and in this sense drama.

3. Programming

Behind the overt physical drama of conversational prayer there is the intellectual drama provided by the programming of the service itself. This is its most potent quality.

The center of this act of worship—which it shares with morning prayer—is the reading of Scripture. The rest of what is done is done in response to that and in amplification of it. The center is not exposition of Scripture. That is, Scripture is not read in order to provide a background for a contemporary exhortation—it is read as a book, as poetry, history, legend, gospel.

Prayers of humble access form the beginning of evensong, but these are among the Reformation additions to it. (They are really appropriate to the assembly of the whole parish at the Mass or Eucharist; in the monastic life "confession" is an altogether separate liturgical activity.) The real "office" begins with the words, "O Lord, open thou our lips," and after the opening responsive sentences of adoration, the reading of Scripture begins at once—with the singing of the appointed section of psalms (broadly speaking, forty or fifty verses at each service). After the reading of the psalms comes the Old Testament reading. That is followed by a choir response in the form of a canticle, the Magnificat, whose inclusion at this point is a truly inspired stroke of drama.

The Magnificat is one of the three songs in the first two chapters of Luke. That section of Scripture, to which only Matthew has anything corresponding, is neither in the Old Testament nor in the New, but right on the boundary between. Christ is not yet born, but he is promised. The point of the Magnificat, then, is not in its violent language, but in the special quality it has in being a lyric poised between the two Testaments. It thrusts us forward toward the reading of the New Testament which follows.

After the New Testament reading comes another song from the same source, the Nunc dimittis. Here we have a song which again is liturgically misunderstood nowadays. It again is a song which looks forward, not backward—in Luke's story it is sung by the priest Simeon while he is holding the infant Christ in his arms. It is dramatically appropriate here because it leads directly to the climax of the service.[5] The center is the reading of Scripture, but the climax is the statement of Christian belief in the creed. After the creed come prayers of intercession, and the

---

[5] I am bound to state my conviction that the singing of the Nunc dimittis at the end of a preaching service or at the end of the Communion service destroys its dramatic sense. The Nunc dimittis comes from the point in history when Jesus was an infant. The New Testament proper is still far ahead. The proper thing to sing at the end of any full public service is a full statement of gospel faith or a hymn which sends people out into the world in a spirit of cheerful resolution. "Mine eyes have seen thy salvation" does not mean "I have seen Christ in my life." It means "I have seen Christ as an infant; I still wait for him to make the promises of God come true." In this opinion I differ, for example, from the compilers of the new Presbyterian liturgy in the U.S.A., who at this point seem to show less than their usual liturgical acumen.

service closes with a greeting—"The grace of the Lord
Jesus Christ. . . ."

Evening prayer must in this sense be seen as the partner
of morning prayer. At morning prayer the other half of the
Scriptures and the psalms is read. At morning prayer also
there is another great Christian affirmation—the *Te Deum.*
The singing of psalms always begins, whatever the day, with
the ninety-fifth, and the New Testament reading is followed by the *Benedictus,* another "frontier" song associated
with the announcement of the coming birth of John the
Baptist—it is this which at morning prayer leads into the
creed.

What needs to be noted here is this: that it is no proper
criticism of morning or evening prayer to examine minutely
the individual words of the canticles and psalms and prayers
that comprise it. The value of the *Magnificat,* the *Nunc
dimittis,* and the *Benedictus* is symbolic. It is a fundamentalist error which dissociates them from this symbolism
and treats them as if they were modern hymns; they are in
the last degree inappropriate to any of the conventional
Reformed services into which they are sometimes intruded.
(They are not in the least inappropriate to services which I
am about to say could be very well used by Reformed
Christians.) But the loss of the sense of drama imparted by
the "frontier" status of the gospel canticles is illustrated at
a very early stage. They are first prescribed for Anglican
services in the Prayer Book of 1549. In the revision of 1552
alternatives are provided for—psalm 100, instead of the
Benedictus, psalm 98 instead of the *Magnificat,* and psalm
67 instead of the *Nunc dimittis.* These cannot be said to be
positively inappropriate, but the demand for them as alternatives was made by puritans who were already doubtful
of the propriety of laying public emphasis on the birth
stories which give prominence to the mother of Christ, and

of the comprehensibility of some of the sentiments contained in them. There is a touch here of that literalism
which was so soon to extrude the sense of drama from public worship in Britain. The inherent dramatic sense of
medieval evensong is at once dimmed when one makes the
puritan substitutions for the canticles.[6]

4. Music

The place of music in this drama is entirely subservient to
the words. In the Middle Ages it was all sung to plainsong—
with variations from one locality to another and other kinds
of variation to mark special high days. Nowadays in cathedrals the music is choral, and congregational participation
is not looked for. But there is one musical reference in the
Prayer Book which is worth a moment's examination,
namely that rubric which directs that "in quires and places
where they sing, here followeth the anthem."

The word "anthem" is derived, not as some have said
from the Greek *anathema* meaning an offering, but from
the English form of a Greek word—*antiphon*, meaning
conversation, or response. An anthem was originally a phrase
of scripture divided for alternate singing by cantor and
choir. It was felt proper by the Prayer Book compilers to
make room in morning and evening prayer for something
which in the Middle Ages had always decorated the order
of the High Mass: namely, a choral, responsive setting of
scriptural words which would mark the day with a certain
individuality. In the prescriptions for the Mass there is a
complete system of "anthems" designed with seasonal
purposes. They are very brief, but most telling in their en-

---

[6] Two other substitutions are of more ancient precedent: the *Benedicite*
instead of the *Te Deum* at morning prayer is in the 1549 Prayer Book.
The "Easter Anthems" in place of the *Venite* did not appear in their
present form until 1662, but the precedent behind them is again an
ancient one.

richment of the worshiper's thought during the service.
(The first one heard on Easter day at Mass, for example,
goes to the words "When I awake, I am still with thee,"
producing an association between psalm 139 and Easter
which in itself adds a new dimension to the drama.)[7]

The purpose of the "anthem," then, is to comment top-
ically, as it were, on the worship, providing a scriptural
bridge between the words of the service and common life for
people whose common life was entirely ruled by the church
seasons. (Ours is ruled by bank holidays and secular tribal
feasts of one kind and another—once again we have to use
imagination to understand worship so deeply rooted in history.)

Naturally, this was the point at which the musician—at
all other points limited to traditional plainsong—was allowed, and welcomed, a measure of freedom. The
"anthems" of the period contemporary with the publication
of the Prayer Book are highly sophisticated and beautiful
settings of the words prescribed for the day, or words
deemed appropriate by the composer. There are many of
these which are now very well-known in churches of all denominations, like Gibbons' "Hosanna to the Son of
David," or Byrd's *Sacerdotes Domini, Hic Dies* and
Justorum animae; but their designed effect was much less
the aesthetic enjoyment which cultivated ears nowadays
take in them, as an enhancement of the drama of the
church's worship. To hear them properly, one needs to
place them dramatically: *Sacerdotes Domini* as an introit,
"Hosanna to the Son of David" as a mid-service anthem on
Palm Sunday, and so on.

When all this is said, perhaps morning and evening
prayer seem still to be a somewhat mild or even inhibited

[7] See Nos. 657 to 734 in the *English Hymnal* for an accessible example
of the anthem system.

form of drama. They have no movement, and they have no audience. The correct comment is, I think, that to those who engage in them they are ceremonial drama—the program building is the drama, and it is entirely familiar; the script is unnecessary except for the anthem. To those who overhear them, they are more than anything else like radio drama—drama for the ear and imagination; drama without scenery or movement or visual force beyond what one gathers from their architectural setting. But in that sense they are "drama of the word," and they were designed to be no more. The very slight content of movement that they have—the rising to the feet for the first "Gloria," the turning to the east (not to face the altar but to get the whole congregation facing the same way, the community in conversation suddenly becoming an army in affirmation) for the creed, are sufficient in themselves to bring the body modestly into the service of the liturgy.

8. drama and the protestants

"Nine Lessons and Carols"

Postponing for the moment any discussion of the dramatic content of the sacraments of the church, let us make some observations in other familiar directions, of services in which the audience's participation is mental rather than physical.

A good example, especially if one remembers its history, is the widespread custom of singing a service of Nine Lessons and Carols at Christmastime. This is a custom which had its modern origin in the inception of the Service of Nine Lessons and Carols held at King's College, Cambridge since 1918,[1] but which has a precedent far more ancient. I choose this service because in some form, both in Britain and in America, it has caught the imagination of so many people who are not of the Anglican way.

The tradition from which it emerges is well exemplified in the service for Passiontide known to Roman Catholics and Anglicans as *Tenebrae*. This is a quite remarkable piece of liturgical drama. It centers on the singing of praise and

---

[1] For some account of the history and development of the service in Cambridge, see my book, *The English Carol*, pp. 227-33 and 245-52.

the reading of Scripture. The scriptures are an extended
passage from Lamentations, Genesis 22, and John 19. Each
reading is divided into three sections.

The readings (nine lessons) are punctuated and surrounded by the singing of psalms. The last psalm is the
Benedictus.

In the center of the chancel, in full view of the worshipers, there is a triangular stand carrying fifteen candles,
all of which are lighted at the beginning of the service, and
one of which is extinguished at the singing of each psalm.
After the *Benedictus* the last candle goes out. In modern
custom the church has its houselights burning so that the
congregation can follow their books, but these are put out
with the last candle, and the church is in darkness. There is
a short prayer, then a period of silence. The directions for
the service then prescribe a harsh sound (*strepitus*)—a person appointed to do it must use any means of making a
shocking and disturbing natural noise in the total darkness.
Then one candle is lit behind the altar, and is brought back
to the stand as the congregation disperses in silence. All
this is enacted on the evening of Good Friday, and is a
simple, profound representation of the death of Christ and
of the promise of his Resurrection. It can be done with a
small choir singing the simplest plainsong, or with elaborate
music (but never with instrumental accompaniment).

That is the origin, or one origin, of the Christmas service
of Nine Lessons and Carols. In the modern service,
naturally, the mood is jubilant, not penitential, and the
festival service is most appropriate when it is held in circumstances as crowded and dignified as those which pertain
to King's College Chapel.

But the Christmas service, as its imitators soon forget,
is based on Scripture, not on music. The musical authorities
at King's have maintained and increased their skill in pro-

viding carols with suitable words as the response to the
Scripture readings, and today it is a peerless example of the
imaginative decoration of the sacred story for the purpose
of bringing it home in contemporary terms.

Now there are certain recognizable ways in which this is
drama.

In the first place, it emerges from human life as human
life is guided and interpreted by the church. This is most
important. Where the drama of the "church's year" has
been lost, this service (like so much else of worship) loses
at once a great deal of its force. The appointed time for
the service is the eve of Christmas. In the church's tradition, Advent is a season of preparation and penitence. Not
until Christmas Eve are Christmas carols sung at all. The
Christmas eve service welcomes the coming of Jesus with
jubilation—but of course, if the season of Advent has been
filled up with carol singing, Christmas parties and whatnot,
as is the universal modern Protestant custom, then the
drama of Christmas Eve falls as flat as a dinner party to
which the guests come full of afternoon tea. What we say
here about the loss of dramatic sense through the neglect
of the church's year applies to all Protestant worship nowadays. Whatever may have been the temporary justification
for the repudiation of the church's year by the English
puritans, its continued neglect is a total disaster for worship. It may be said (as some are now saying) that social
changes are making necessary some adjustments to the
traditional pattern; these would be welcome if they brought
back the sense that all through the year, over and over
again, we are taking part in the Christian drama of salvation even before we have set foot in church.

Secondly, the carol service derives dramatic content from
the sequence of thought that runs through the readings
and carols. The first reading is the story of the Fall in

Genesis 3; the last is the mighty metaphysic of the prologue to John. Between them come the prophecies and the birth legends. The sensitiveness of the contemporary authorities at Cambridge ordains that the opening reading shall be preceded by the hymn, "Of the Father's love begotten," a very ancient mythological hymn containing a reference to the Fall:

> He assumed this mortal body,
> Frail and feeble, doomed to die,
> That the race from dust created
> Might not perish utterly
> Which the dreadful law had sentenced
> In the depths of hell to lie

and followed by the carol, "Adam lay ybounden." The same authority decrees that John's prologue be followed by the one really well-known metaphysical hymn, "O come, all ye faithful":

> God of God,
> Light of light,
> Lo, he abhors not the virgin's womb;
> Very God
> Begotten, not created. . . .
>
> Yea, Lord, we greet thee,
> Born this happy morning,
> Jesus, to thee be all glory given;
> Word of the Father,
> Now in flesh appearing.

Of the use of mythological and credal language of this kind I shall say a little more in a moment. But any careful study of this service will show how delicately the drama is worked out through the means available.

Now here the one thing that is absent altogether is anything corresponding to the candles and the harsh noise at *Tenebrae*. (One feels that the one thing that would defeat the choir of King's College would be the demand for a harsh noise.) But the richness of the music, and the inspiriting words of the carols, provide enough drama to catch the imagination of a whole nation—which is what this service in fact has done. It therefore provides a suitable introduction to the somewhat knotty problem which we must now take up.

Drama of the Mind

I have nothing here to say about the abuses, disorder, sentimentality, and banality into which the Protestant service so often falls. Enough has been said already by others about this.[2] And anyhow I have said nothing about the intolerable casualness that can overtake an Anglican evensong when it is badly produced, or the hectic and ill-organized charade that a carol service can become. But I must make the point that even those who follow the puritan tradition that produced Prynne's notorious outburst in 1633 against the theater, and produced later the Victorian paterfamilias who told his children that all stage plays were of the devil, have been unable entirely to extrude drama from their worship. They did what they could. The deliberate rejection of the custom of keeping the church's year, as we have already said, was a major blow against drama—at a stroke it cut off worship from society. It implied a total rejection of the medieval view of the church as a force which unobtrusively but irresistibly permeated all life. There is a kind of a priori receptiveness in the worshiper who, coming to church, knows that the day of his worship is the second Sunday in

[2] For example (and not at all from the point of view that I am taking here), Geddes Macgregor in *The Coming Reformation* (Philadelphia: The Westminster Press, 1960).

Advent, or the Sunday after the Ascension, and therefore knows something of what he is to expect in the worship, in contrast to the worshiper who comes entirely unprepared for what will take place. The rejection also of *movement* in worship—no processions, no movement of the minister from stall to lectern, from altar to chancel step, no movement of the congregation even to the Communion rail, not even any custom of kneeling for prayer—removed another channel through which drama could be enacted. But even so, the puritan forms of worship sought to involve the congregation, and this, being cut off from other means, they had to do by three methods only: the use of abounding eloquence, the use of mental involvement through concentrated attention, and the assumption that the congregation was not merely a family at worship, but a very obedient, receptive, and expectant family.

The Drama of Rhetoric

A puritan preacher like Baxter, for example, involved his congregation by demanding, and getting from them, a supreme mental effort. In his day there was nothing else that made this demand. Meeting the demand satisfactorily was an achievement which paid dividends in intellectual satisfaction and in the enjoyment of the drama of eloquence. A kind of dramatic "preparation" was provided by the atmosphere of persecution and illicitness which surrounded the seventeenth-century puritans after the Restoration in England. The gradual removal of this incentive to drama corresponded with the increase of eloquence in the preacher at the expense of that intellectual integrity and ruthlessness which characterizes the twenty, thirty, and fifty-point locutions of Baxter. Where the worshiping congregation gathered illicitly, there was already as good a preparation for drama as the church's year had provided in

the days of faith. When this was relaxed, the characteristic
quality of the successful preacher had to be a gift for rousing
people from inertia, an increasing use of the minatory note,
more frequent references to the divine wrath, more devices
for awakening people from sleep. Therefore, as time went
on, the preacher became more openly an actor, more
skilled in the arts of rhetoric. The Methodists (though not
primarily John Wesley, who by all accounts was an old-
fashioned, level-headed puritan when he was preaching)
taught Englishmen and Americans these arts very ably.
Fringe Anglicans who embraced the evangelical way spread
the skill among their own people. The doctrines of Calvin,
more particularly that of predestination, provided ideal
material for drama in preaching; therefore the churches
which were least liturgical in their habits had to be the most
rhetorical, and by a process of assimilation became the
most Calvinistic.

But the art of rhetoric can become a species of entertainment. The ingredients of high tragedy are all there in the
material from which the famous preachers from Jonathan
Edwards to Joseph Parker drew their fire. But just as the
great romantic vocabulary in music lent itself to facile
misuse, so did the violent dissonances of Calvinist preaching. It could be rather entertaining to be dangled over the
bottomless pit by an able rhetorician. Where the older
puritans could be ruthless, the later ones verged on sentimentality. But none of them could do without drama.

The Fading of Drama

What we have not fully realized in our own time where
we continue to hold services in which preaching is central
is what kind of drama is appropriate to our situation. That
is why a historical sensitiveness to the progress of drama
in puritan worship is of vital importance to us now. We

have to be alert on the one hand to the drama that the world outside provides, and on the other to that which we are called on to provide. Here we have three periods—a period in which there is, or is assumed to be, persecution outside; a period in which there is peace outside; and a period in which there is a revolution outside. Persecution outside causes the family inside the church to close the doors and worship as a tightly knit community. The drama is produced by the critical encounter between the Gospel and life in the unfriendly world; it is near enough to the conditions in which the New Testament was written to provide its own motive power. Apathy or negative peace outside produces a demand for high mental drama within, best furnished by dramatic Calvinist preaching. But what we have not come to terms with is the situation of the church in a world where there is just too little natural drama to go around. Even in what we call the times of apathy or negative peace there was a good deal more death, poverty, hunger, and war within the experience of the worshiping Christian we are talking about than there is now. There was plenty of social outlet for Christian indignation, reforming zeal, and sense of discontent. Compared with the nineteenth century, our own provides insufficient outlets for Christian concern in the immediate neighborhood of the worshiper. This may seem a surprising suggestion in a time of such abundant moralizing and scolding as the present, but I doubt if it can seriously be challenged. Death came into every home in 1850, especially infant death. Poverty was evident in every town. Death and poverty are largely removed from the sight of ordinary worshipers now. What the worshiper knows, he knows of as other people's troubles: people dying in hospitals; accidents on the road in other people's cars; wars in other countries; race riots in other states; hunger and poverty on other continents.

Hectoring voices bemuse him with demands for his concern over people who are not in the "good Samaritan" sense his neighbors. The connection between the drama of life and the drama of worship is at present, for the Protestant, in a state of complete disorganization. Equally for the Catholic, the connection between the drama of secular life and the drama of liturgy is becoming sufficiently widely doubted to give rise to a great deal of impatience with traditional liturgical forms.

From the other side it is easy to see, and I hope I have shown how the "inside" drama corresponds to a period of persecution or a period of peace in a society where nature in its malignant and violent forms is still not far away. A family at worship behind closed doors can play at charades or engage in a kind of socio-drama. Puritan worship is socio-drama or charade rather than scripted drama, but so long as there is sufficient intimacy for everybody to know his part, or to be relied on to improvise it harmoniously, the thing will work. The historic puritans were too sensitive about all the other arts (pictorial or dramatic) to make any use of them in worship; but they did use music (and indeed they enjoyed and performed music in their own homes). Their use of music was often a kind of rude socio-drama, or even charade. The prejudice among English Baptists of the mid-seventeenth century against the use of hymnbooks indicates a suspicion of what could not be done with an appearance of spontaneity; a similar indication comes of their predilection for prayer that was, or appeared to be, extempore. A kind of drama which you made up as you went along was appropriate when secular life had adequately prepared you for it, and when the "cast" knew each other well enough to be able to do this very elementary kind of "speaking with tongues" intelligibly to one another. It is equally easy to see how a one-man proscenium entertainment was appropriate to a time when congregations were larger, intimacy had dispersed, and "charade" was impossible. In such a case the drama must be more public, more clearly directed. If it were not "scripted" by a prayerbook, then it must be "produced" by the genius of the presiding minister.

And that is where, in the more peaceful areas of Protestantism, we still are. It is not, of course, where they are in the places where racial tension has produced a new sense of persecution and even personal suffering. It is not where they are in places where the equilibrium of society has suffered real shocks. It is no accident at all that the closed communities of Negro worshipers are given to highly demonstrative worship, or that the new pentecostal explosion originated from downtown Los Angeles. What I am saying here applies to such congregations as that only insofar as it shows how drama, or a sense of crisis, in secular life injects drama into worship.

The Catholics can still basically turn to their liturgies; but the Protestants are entirely uneasy about their forms of worship, and this is why. There seems to be very little connection between a reasonably prosperous and well-ordered service of Protestant worship and anything whatever. If the sermon is central, we now ask what question in the common life of the worshiper it is supposed to be answering. Is it ever anything more than the posing of a dummy-question, and the answering of it by a speaker whose skill need be only great enough to demolish his own imaginary arguments? Is not preaching like so much contemporary Christian action—a frantic search for something wrong that somebody can get satisfaction from in putting right?

The one thing that can be done with a normal Protestant service is to see that, at least at the level of mental drama, and if at all possible at a more visible level than that, it has integrity and sense. A Protestant service is, from one to the next, a new creation. It is strictly existential. It is an occasion when the eternal gospel is made new not only in preaching but also in the ordering of every word, including especially the choice of the congregational hymns. The ideal choice of hymn, psalm, or anthem, is that which puts in the congregation's mouth the very word it was waiting to express. There is (need it be said?) no case whatever for tying down the worship of any Protestant church to an order of service which, throughout the year, never varies. I can only express my astonishment that churches affluent enough to provide printed bulletins for the congregation every Sunday of the year take no opportunity of varying the order of service. Unvarying orders result in a needless restriction of the subject matter, the hymns and psalms sung, and the anthems rendered by the choir; or else in the constant interruption of the natural drama of the service (which should be basically the drama of Scripture) by irrelevant and distracting choir pieces and congregational hymns. Even where there is no initial opportunity of introducing any drama of movement, one can at least be sure that the thought pattern of the service, from which the dramatic impact throughout the congregation will come, is continuous from its opening to its end, that the hymns reinforce it and do not distract the congregation's mind from it, and that anthems are sung only at that point in each service where they will equally contribute to it. A service is not gathered around a single thought that the preacher has invented. It is a progressive drama in which everything has its proper place, and which misplacements will destroy at a touch.

Before coming to a conclusion about this, allow me to illustrate once more from a known form of worship— namely, Benjamin Britten's church opera, *Noye's Fludde*.

9. the theater of faith

Noye's Fludde

Noye's Fludde, by Benjamin Britten (Op. 59, 1958), is a setting to music of a medieval church play. One of the most attractive things about medieval church practice was the way in which, though it scorned the sermon, it found means of making the Bible come alive for the common people, who were so largely illiterate. The stained-glass windows in their churches were their visual aids—pictures of biblical characters of stories; and their plays, acted in church or taken around the countryside on wagons rather in the manner of a modern carnival, reminded the people of the great stories and principles of their faith. This play is of this kind, and is simply a reenactment of the tale of Noah.

Basically it is a charade involving a few adults and a large number of children, in which we see Noah being commanded to build the ark, and actually building it; the creatures of the earth, represented by children wearing headdresses suggestive of animal heads, go into the ark, represented by a tiered stand on the "stage"; the storm rises and subsides, the raven and the dove are sent out from the ark (children again, this time ballet dancers), and the whole company of creatures leave the vessel again with alleluias.

The music is very simple, played by a small orchestra including strings, recorders, percussion, a trumpet, and a piano. The percussion section includes a set of tin mugs to be tapped with spoons. All the music can be played by decently disposed amateurs. The whole play is sung from beginning to end, and it includes imaginative decorations of the story: Noah's conversations with his family, Mrs. Noah's reluctance to leave her friends (her "gossips") and enter the ark at all (which anyhow she doesn't believe will be safe), and other homely details of that kind.

The play is designed to be put on in an ordinary church. Simple scenery only is required. The original setting was one of those majestic parish churches in East Anglia, but the first performance I saw happened to be in a Scottish Presbyterian church of uncompromisingly nineteenth-century design, and even there the whole affair is entirely convincing.

The congregational participation is confined to three hymns, which are perfectly normal hymns found in most English hymnbooks. They are of the greatest importance to the whole scheme, both musically and because of their words. I want especially to attend to the hymns here, because it is out of these that the particular point I want to make emerges.

This is the full text of the first hymn, which is the opening of the play.

> Lord Jesus, think on me,
> And purge away my sin;
> From earthborn passions set me free
> And make me pure within.
>
> Lord Jesus, think on me,
> Nor let me go astray,
> Through darkness and perplexity
> Point thou the heavenly way.

> Lord Jesus, think on me,
>   When flows the tempest high;
> When on doth rush the enemy,
>   O Saviour, be thou nigh.
>
> Lord Jesus, think on me,
>   That, when the flood is past,
> I may th'eternal brightness see
>   And share thy joy at last.

And this is the tune:

Fig. 18   Southwell

In the words of the hymn, observe the following points of appropriateness:

(1) It is a well-known hymn to English congregations (especially to Anglican ones with whom the composer is primarily familiar). It is a very ancient hymn, from a Greek original composed in the fourth century. It has been in English hymnbooks for a little over a hundred years.

(2) As a church folk song, it is associated with the season of Lent. Like all hymns rich in the mythology of that season, its primary subject is spiritual danger; it is somewhat broader than moral temptation—it pictures the Tempter as a positive principle of evil.

(3) Therefore it gathers up the traditional interpretation of the flood as a manifestation of God's anger, and of its subsiding as the token of God's forgiveness. All this was

familiar to the worshiper (as the composer assumes) before
he came into church. It all comes back to him as the hymn
starts. He says, as it were, "Ah! that good old hymn: danger;
forgiveness; Jesus!"

(4) But especially it happens to mention the flood; it
does not mention the flood in the Greek original, but in
this translation it associates it (as does Charles Wesley's
famous "Jesu, lover of my soul") with the story of Noah.
So at once the special image is impressed on the worshiper's
mind.

The tune is a psalm tune first printed before 1600, exceedingly simple and musically eloquent. It is unusual
among psalm tunes in making a special use of repeated
notes. The composer extracts from it two basic musical
points (marked in the music as examples A and B) out of
which he fashions the main musical motifs of the whole
piece—for example in this phrase in which the chorus expresses its dismay at the gathering storm:

Fig. 19

Ah greate God, that arte so good, that worckës not thy will is wood,

Now all this worlde is on a flude, as I see will in sighte.

Reprinted with permission of Boosey & Hawkes Music Publishers Ltd.

The second hymn comes at the climax, where the storm
is raging and all the creatures are settled in the ark. The
storm itself is represented by a long *passacaglia* by the
orchestra, rising in a general crescendo interrupted by oc-

casional falls in volume.[1] At the very height of this, when
the orchestra is blowing and hammering with every muscle,
the whole cast on stage breaks in with the hymn, "Eternal
Father, strong to save." The second verse is sung by the
congregation with the cast, over a continuing *ostinato*
orchestral "storm bass"; the third verse is sung by all present
to the hymn tune as it was originally written, accompanied
by the organ.

The dramatic content of this breaks down as follows:

(1) "Eternal Father, strong to save" is *the* sailors' hymn
in Great Britain. (It was sung at the signing of the Atlantic
Charter.) It is almost one of the national anthems. If anybody knows five hymns, that will be one of them. The
congregation is therefore brought in with something that
for a hundred years has been entirely its own.

(2) You might say that there could be few greater in-
congruities than the working of a tune by J. B. Dykes into
a Benjamin Britten score. But there is no incongruity—the
whole play is reaching out so far toward the audience that
it seems the most natural thing in the world for them to
come in with this hymn, and *this tune*. The tune is naïvely
dramatic, and it happens, at its climactic point, to introduce
exactly the same motif of repeated notes that appeared in
the old psalm tune (compare A and B in **Fig. 20**). So not
only is the merest folk singer in the congregation gathered
up—there is something for the musical imagination as well.

(3) The most important thing, however, is this: that, instructed briefly in a written program, the worshiping congregation is warned to expect this hymn and to join in.
All through the playing of the storm music, the worshipers

---

[1] This is not only a perfectly natural representation of the rise and fall
in the gathering of a storm, but also a remarkably close reflection of the
tensional variations in the most famous of all *passacaglias*, J. S. Bach's C
minor for organ (S. 582).

are edging toward the fronts of their seats, waiting for the
moment when they leap to their feet and join in the hymn.
The hymn is precisely what they want to say. No other
hymn would have done. It is a great hymn here just because it is popular; it is easy to join in, and when they do
join in, the worshipers bring all their own traditional experience to bear on the drama. When the third verse is
sung with the organ, making exactly the same noise that it
makes whenever it is sung in an ordinary service, the normal
worship of the church is locked securely into the drama
that is being played. Noah comes up to date. The flood is
now—the danger and the forgiveness are *now*.

(This is not the first time a hymn has been brought into
a church score—remember the hymns in the Bach passions,
which were designed toward exactly the same effect. But
contrast the hymn at the end of Gustav Holst's miracle play
—words by John Masefield—"The Coming of Christ." It is
a marvelous hymn in respect of both words and tune—but
nobody knows it unless there has been a very full congregational rehearsal—and anyhow, nobody has known it ever
since he was born, and can say that his grandfather knew it.
It simply is not congregational participation in the sense
that Britten's use of "Eternal Father" is.)

The last hymn is at the end of the play, and it is Joseph
Addison's "The spacious firmament," sung to Tallis' famous
Canon. All is now over. The rainbow is shining, the storm
is past, and the land is dry. No words could express the
sense of peace and well-being that is wanted here as well as
Addison's hymn. It is a difficult hymn to use in ordinary
worship—it is pure eighteenth-century "Cosmic Toryism,"
"All's right with the world" theology—and one has to be
careful how one tries to integrate it into a normal service.
But here it is exactly right. It is simple; it is even incom-
plete. The peace it expresses is, if you like, unregenerate.

But dramatically it expresses what those animals and that family felt in the story of Noah, and that is what it is doing there. And once again the tune is a folk song of the church. It is virtually certain that the play will be put on in the afternoon or evening, so there is no incongruity in its close association with the evening hymn "All praise to thee, my God, this night." It is solid, unpretentious, ancient, and known to everybody. And as if that were not enough, it has a triumphant musical congruity with our key phrase in the repeated notes of its second line (**Fig. 20, C**):

Fig. 20

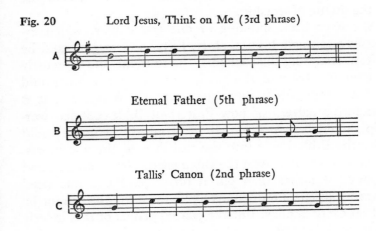

Lord Jesus, Think on Me (3rd phrase)

A

Eternal Father (5th phrase)

B

Tallis' Canon (2nd phrase)

C

I do not think that it is difficult to see that here we have the "missing link" in contemporary worship. A study of the use of these three hymns in *Noye's Fludde* is a sufficient education in how to choose hymns for public worship. Basically, and making every allowance for the need to get a sufficient number of hymns known to a congregation to make this possible, this is how hymns should be chosen: with a sensitive ear to their allusions (especially to cross-references like that to the flood in the first of these), a neighborly concern that they shall be practically singable, and a very careful use of the hymns that people regard as "their own," and that make it possible for them really to bring part of themselves into the drama of worship. A hymn is not "their own" until it is really well known, almost hackneyed. During the earlier stages a new hymn is part of the drama that is coming across from the pulpit-end of the church—when it is really a folk song, it is part of the drama that comes from the pew-end. That is the secret that ministers and directors of worship and organists must master before the choosing of hymns becomes a real part of the drama of worship.

We have been speaking of one single play, which expresses one single biblical story. Fifty more pages could be written analyzing the economy, the restraint, the supremely congruous artistry of this work. But the conclusion would be the same: this is how to present the Bible, and it is therefore a pattern of how Protestant Bible-centered worship should be conceived. If we would preach, we would drive the Bible home into the real lives of the worshipers. Even if all we do is read the Bible rather than acting it, and expound it rather than put it on stage, the drama need never be absent. Productions like *Noye's Fludde* cannot be put on every Sunday. But the central genius of it is exactly what every worship director who knows his business has been trying to apply through all the generations of Protestantism. And if this means that the conventional choir anthems must go, or be looked at in quite a new light, then that is a conclusion which we ought to be willing to accept. The one thing that you do not think of for a moment at a performance of *Noye's Fludde* is a concert of classical music. That is why it is a far more powerful contribution to the ongoing life of the church than are many more elaborate masterpieces, such even as Britten's *War*

Requiem. *Noye's Fludde* is the same stuff as the Bach Passions, but not really the same stuff as Handel's *Messiah*.

The Drama of the Upper Room

It was necessary to leave until now the most obvious piece of evidence to support our argument, because to introduce it earlier would have induced a false sense of security in the reader. Christian worship is, as everybody knows, founded in a dramatic action known as the Eucharist, the Mass, the Holy Communion, or the Lord's Supper. Sacramental worship is worship assisted by physical action. In the two Gospel sacraments generally recognized by Protestants, and in the five others recognized by Catholics, the prerequisite of a sacrament is an "outward and visible sign of an inward and spiritual grace"; and that sign, being outward and visible, is physical. The Christian communions differ, however, not only in their outward forms of worship but in the image which the *signs* in the sacraments are deemed to unveil.

To some, the Lord's Supper is a "family meal," just as public worship is essentially "family prayers"—all the associations that gather around the family are to some degree present: the closed door, the initiation, the close fellowship of believers with one another. To others the primary image is "sacrifice" with its attendant notions of universality, objectivity, and openness. (A sacrifice in the times of the Old Testament could be offered as appropriately in the open air as indoors, and could never be offered in a private house.) In either case, the physical bread and wine make the historical connection between the service and its inception, but in the ordinary man's worship the real difference between the denominations is not doctrinal but rather in the difference between the drama which the Catholic believes he is enacting and that which the Protestant thinks he is enacting. The subject may be the same but there are two entirely different scripts.

This is not the kind of thing one can extract from a study of parallel confessions or documents of church order. But it is much nearer the thoughts that ordinary worshipers are thinking. There is a fascinating passage in one of the essays in Nathaniel Micklem's book, *My Cherry Tree*, which nicely illustrates this point. The passage begins: "I, who am an unrepenting (though dissatisfied) Protestant believe the doctrine of transubstantiation, and the majority of Roman Catholics do not." He continues:

I affirm that most Roman Catholics do not believe this dogma because it is a highly philosophical theory which they are quite incapable of understanding; and I am prepared to affirm that I believe it, because if one can by an exercise of historic imagination bring oneself to think in the old terms of substance and accident, which the dogma presupposes, then I think the matter must be put as this dogma puts it.[2]

This is right. The heirs of that Reformation, one of whose main contentions was against a *doctrine*, are in fact Protestants now not because they hold, or are interested one way or the other in, the doctrine, but because they are following a different script. I know no other way of putting it. All churches which celebrate the Communion service at all agree that they are in some sense doing what Jesus did and what he told them to do; and yet people of different traditions differ widely in what they think *they* are doing.

In the English country parish church, the worshiper goes to the Communion rail at an early hour on Sunday morning, in the course of a service which is entirely spoken, and,

[2] From "The Church Apostolic and Apostatic" (New York: William Collins Sons & Co., 1966), p. 52.

as he says, he "makes his Communion." This is a highly personal act of communion between him and his Lord. In a sung Eucharist in the Church of England, there is the music to give the congregation an added sense of togetherness; in the High Mass there is much drama at the altar, and on special days even among the people by way of processions. Traditionally the Mass may not be associated with personal communion at all. There is drama here, and mystery, and a considerable emphasis on sacrifice. In a Protestant church of the dissenting kind there is very little mystery, very little movement, the people remain in their seats and are either served by deacons or (as some of us think preferable) serve one another with the sacred Elements. Commonly one or both of the Elements are retained so that all may eat or drink together. The sense of community is here paramount. The notion of "sacrifice" has disappeared. It is a family meal, served from a table, not a sacrifice offered on an altar. And even if there are doctrinal disputes between one body and another over such matters as sacrifice and transubstantiation, it is not these which express the real differences. It is not because of a doctrine that an Anglican feels out of place at a Dissenting table, or a Dissenter at an Anglican one. It is not a doctrine that causes the Church of England and the Roman Catholic Church to provide in urban parishes a Communion on almost every day of the year, and the Church of Scotland to celebrate once every three months. What people are accustomed to doing, and are brought up to do, in their churches, seems to them to be the natural outcome of the way they look at the church, at its worship, and at one another at least as much as the outcome of doctrines. Doctrines are most often used in discussion to rationalize these differences; when they are claimed to be their origin, unreality at once falls on the discussions. This happens to be one of the matters not very much canvased in the public statements associated with the ecumenical movement. The Protestant at a Catholic Mass may say "I don't like that," but what he means is "It does not occur to me to do that."

Churchmen have, I suspect, been unwilling to look at things this way because they are shy of attaching any importance to the notion that in worship "we" are doing anything at all. The assumption often is that it is God who acts, and God alone. This is pious talk, nothing more. Nobody who really has anything actively to do with public worship believes it. Of course the preacher, the organist, the choir, the assistants, the church keeper are "doing something." What matters is to persuade the Protestant worshiper that he is doing something.

Without making any comment on doctrine, then, except to observe that perverse doctrine can be expected to issue from perverse behavior (as well as the converse), I suggest that the unquestionable disappearance of the Sacraments from the consciousness of so many pious Protestants —nowhere more clearly visible than in Scotland and in those places where Scottish religious culture has become normative—is chiefly due to the alignment of all worship with a personally inhibited and cowed attitude toward God and his works. It is altogether too clear to go unnoticed, that those who value the Sacraments most, and who surround them with the greatest content both of penitence and joy, are also those who accept dramatic movement in church. Processions, lights, symbolic movements of all kinds are of the Catholic culture; immobility of congregation and minister is of the Protestant culture; and which of these is it that takes the more homely and innocent *pleasure* in the ordinance of Christ?

Music at the Eucharist

In the use of music in the service of the Lord's Supper (in any case the only Sacrament with which music can be extensively associated), the first necessity is to discover which script you are using. There will probably be little disagreement with the statement that if you would see church music doing its work unobtrusively yet powerfully, efficiently and with true congregational acceptance, a choral Eucharist with plainsong and two or three congregational hymns is about as good a pattern as you could find. One sees the proper and original use here of the "anthem" (see above, p. 143), a great deal of congregational participation, a great deal of music that is entirely familiar, the "contemporizing" of the liturgy through the judicious use of modern lyrics and music, the distinction of high days in the church's year by the use of more decorative and assertive music, and with all this the restrained, deliberate and precisely calculated movements of the celebrants. This may not be what everybody is used to; but at least you can see, even "from outside," what is supposed to be happening. There is no reason at all why Protestant services of the kind should not be just as "good theater"; but in order to make them so, a quite new attitude to, and freedom of, physical movement, congregational response, and the use of the church building is the first requirement.

The liturgy of the Church of South India is a godsend to Protestants—for although it savors so much of the Anglican rite, it is used by a church with which the major Protestant denominations are avowedly in communion. In many churches that is a good place to start. And yet even this is not the whole story. The great innovation, for most of us, in the South India service is the "kiss of peace," where members of the congregation take one another by the hand as a sacramental vow of fellowship; this is an action which comes as strangely to the "private" Anglican communicant as to the "family meal" Dissenter. And indeed a good exercise in church music practical studies would be to work out a system of contemporary church music which could provide a suitable musical adornment for the South India liturgy celebrated in Western countries. But even so we have to add that to "lay on" such a service in a church accustomed to worship of a quite different sort is not of any real value unless a sense of drama has already been awakened in the worshiping community; and if it has been, then it will already have begun to extract the drama from underneath the conventional inactivity of its own tradition.

V
church music
transformed

10. drama and church music

We began with a tag from Tillich about Emotion, Knowledge, and Will; Tillich used the tripartite pattern to explain erroneous attitudes toward biblical theology, and I ventured to use it to describe the special qualities, and therefore occasionally the errors, of the church music of the last few generations. We are now moving toward a conclusion in which that pattern can helpfully be recalled. The dangers which show themselves through overemphasis in different kinds of church music (the Victorian, emphasizing emotion and the present; the Edwardian, knowledge, pedagogy, and the past; the contemporary, will, rebellion, and the future) show themselves in human psychology. But the church's business at worship is to show the whole man to himself, and to call forth the gifts and the responses of the whole man. I have indicated that this will be possible only if the church's worship is seen to be essentially not merely experience, not merely instruction, not merely an appeal to the will, but a drama which includes all these things and fuses them into a living whole. My contention is that drama does include all these things; I am saying not that worship should be replaced by what we narrowly call

173

"drama," but that worship is the authentic kind of drama; and if it tries not to be drama, it is false to itself and its basic purposes.

Return to the New Testament

Virtually nothing is said in the New Testament about how the church ought to worship. There is plenty in the Old Testament about how Jews should do it, but Christians have no instructions. The very few things that are said about worship are all said by Paul, and are all said in his first letter to Corinth; they all not only support but positively prescribe the approach which I am asking for here.

There is a passage in I Corinthians 11 concerning the Communion Service, or Eucharist—the passage which contains the venerable Words of Institution which the church universally uses at that observance. This is not a liturgical prescription, but a protest against the sordid habits of the people at Corinth, who made the Christian meeting an occasion for treating one another badly.

> Your meetings tend to do more harm than good. . . . I am told that when you meet as a congregation you fall into sharply divided groups. . . . The result is that . . . it is impossible for you to eat the Lord's Supper, because each of you is in such a hurry to eat his own, and while one goes hungry another has too much to drink. (I Cor. 11:17-21 NEB.)

It is just after that passage that the "Words of Institution" appear in the text. The error of Corinth was not in any liturgical fault, but at the more human level of plain bad manners—it was not in what they said but in what they did.

A little later, in chapter 14, the apostle has a passage about the misuse of "spiritual gifts," in which he warns the

church members against the "language of ecstasy" which is
unintelligible to its hearers. If intellect is banished, the acts
of worship in such a community as that are useless. The
whole passage is worth quoting at length—but I venture
to think that a slight amendment of the accepted translation, doing no violence at all to the Greek text, will bring
out more forcibly the exact point that Paul is making. He
is contrasting the "speaker with tongues" with the prophet.
The prophet is a good communicator; the ecstatic speaker
is usually a bad one.

Prophecy must be distinguished from the speech of ecstasy.
Prophecy builds men up; it comforts and encourages them.
Ecstatic speech is good for the speaker, no doubt; but it is
prophecy that builds up the church. I am willing that you
should all speak ecstatically, but I would rather that you
prophesied. The prophet is worth more than the ecstatic
speaker, unless he explains himself and so gives the church the
chance to benefit from what he says. Well then, my friends:
if I come to you speaking ecstatically, what use shall I be
to you if what I say does not have in it some revelation, some
knowledge, some prophecy, or some teaching?
Even lifeless things have voices—like the oboe or the guitar;
but if there is no clear distinction between the sounds of the
instruments, how will a man know whether it is an oboe or
a guitar that is being played? If the trumpet does not make
a clear trumpet-sound, who will prepare for war? [1]

(I Cor. 14:4-8, author's translation)

In both passages Paul is in different ways pleading for a
complete meeting, or communication, between persons.
This is why his fourteenth chapter follows inevitably and
naturally after his more celebrated thirteenth. Love is the

---

[1] For "guitar," see above, p. 95. "Flute" is a clear mistranslation of
the Greek aulos, which was a reed instrument.

primary spiritual gift and the primary fabric of the human community. Secondary gifts are secondary because they are capable of being so misused as to contradict love. But what is love without communication, or meeting? The love of which Paul speaks in I Corinthians 13 is not the love which makes two people one *flesh* (that is *eros*); but it is the love that absorbs differences between personalities, and makes a community something more than an aggregation of separate persons. So communication in church worship—whether through the care of persons whose lack he deplores in chapter 11 or through the care of minds whose lack he deplores in chapter 14—is a function of love. When it breaks down, he says, we see what happens; people accentuate social differences at the Lord's Supper, and in worship meetings talk for their own satisfaction and nobody else's benefit. It is always relevant to ask, in any Christian community today, how far we have gone in the direction of both these errors. If we do ask such questions we shall suddenly see an alarming fact which normally we allow to hide itself from us; namely, that a great deal of institutional worship is a matter of segregating like-minded (and, let us face it, like-incomed and like-born) people, and of providing contexts in which people can talk at length for their own satisfaction and nobody's edification without incurring blame or ridicule.

This is all the New Testament has to tell us about worship—apart from certain comments of our Lord, preserved in Matthew 6, about loveless worship which in the end provide the primary authority for the passages we have just been observing. It is all—but it is quite enough. Worship is a function of love, and its communications, personal and intellectual, must not frustrate it.

My contention is that this means drama.

Misconceptions Removed

This is the connection: that "drama," properly understood, means the only way in which a community can
achieve a corporate response to the fundamental data of
life. For Christians the fundamental datum is God; but the
august name of God must not make Christians shy of responding through drama. If necessary we must simply re-
define drama.

The difficulty in using the word is in keeping it clear of
secondary associations. People will react to propositions
such as I have been making as though we were saying that
the Christian faith is something like a play by St. John
Ervine—devised for the entertainment and comfort of the
socially assured and secure. The essence of drama is not in
the entertainment of a passive audience, but in the involvement of a community in a total response to the fundamental data.

This is why Greek drama in the fifth century B.C. was
an expression of religion. It is the best example in history
of a community's corporate response to the fundamental
data through plays. In the aesthetically sophisticated community of fifth-century Athens, drama did more for community religion than any more officially religious observance,
except only the "mysteries" of Eleusis—and what were
these but another form of drama? But every religion, as
any student of comparative religions knows, has drama at
the center of its observances, and this drama ultimately
falls into two categories: sex drama and war drama (or,
in other words, nature drama and conflict drama). The
Christian archetypal drama is an exaltation of both: the
nature drama of baptism and the Lord's Supper, and the
conflict drama of the cross and resurrection. Our Lord is
represented in the Gospels in the twofold role of the Lord
of Creation (through his mastery over nature) and the

Captain of Salvation (through his submission to and transformation of its most potent force—death).

Impediments to Drama

As I have already suggested, the worst impediment to a proper use of music and the arts in church today is a commitment to pedagogy allied with a commitment to Western bourgeois Protestant conventions. The more Protestant the church, the heavier the commitment becomes. The more Protestant the church, the worse "theater" its worship usually makes, the more likely it is that its members will tend to religious exclusiveness and that its preaching will be esoteric and, in Paul's sense, ecstatic.

I am sure that when Peter saw the vision of that great bag coming down from heaven with all the animals (pigs included) in it (Acts 10), and heard a voice from heaven making him free of everything he could see, he was being told that his business, as a key figure in the church, was not to confine the gospel to telling the Jews how wrong they had been (which according to his biographer Luke he had never lost an opportunity of doing), but that he must expand his communication to welcome people like the centurion Cornelius who within a few minutes would be knocking at his door. You do not communicate eternal truth to Cornelius by telling him that the Jews were wrong to crucify Jesus; but that is just the kind of error which the church, especially when it overlooks the universal hazards of the arts, continues to commit. This is misplaced pedagogy.

Application to Music

It happens that at present music is the most pedagogic of the arts. Music teaching is an expanding industry. Music is the nearest thing among the arts to a school subject in its own right. (In schools you do not specifically "teach" poetry, architecture, sculpture, or drama to children of twelve, although you do teach what is called "art," meaning drawing; and the teaching of this is not so regimented as the teaching of music.) The current attitude toward "good" music is a much more pronounced attitude, something much more closely associated with a set of social values, than current attitudes to the other arts. With music everything that gathers round the other arts to some extent in the way of social attitudes becomes much more explicit. Music is also the only art, apart from that of rhetoric, which the Reformed churches take with any seriousness, or accept without a priori criticism.

Therefore the first necessity is to abolish altogether the idea of pure "listener's music" from the activities of the church. In our secular attitudes to concert music we need in any case to become more self-conscious. It would be nonsense to say that there should be no more public performances of Beethoven and Brahms and Tchaikovsky; all we need is to take a less optimistic view of their automatic capacities for benefit. "Love of music" can be abused just as "love of the brethren" was abused in I Corinthians 11. It can be difficult for some kinds of people to accept and value other kinds of people whose musical values differ, and whose values in other fields differ also. This is the great pitfall that lies before the feet of the church music reformer. At this time, when music-making is such a widespread activity, and such a developing industry, the puritan values need to be revived. A certain self-criticism is necessary for those who would promote in church the use of music which carries strong suggestions of the concert hall and of the classics. I myself must confess that I cannot arouse any great enthusiasm for performances of cantatas by the incomparable Bach unless they are very clearly integrated with a "worship script" which does not stop at saying that because

Bach's music is good, therefore this is a valid act of worship. Still less would I value the performance of choral anthems merely for the sake of giving the congregation a chance to listen passively to music. If it is excellent music, perhaps less damage is done than if it is dreadful music; but even so the efficiency level of this activity for producing what worship is supposed to produce is very low.

But the trouble is not in the music; it is in those who use it. It is not the composer's fault—it is the fault of those who will strike attitudes about "good" music. For no true work of art is designed merely to confirm a social attitude; it is not even designed merely to arouse a passive listener to assent. It is designed to involve a listener or a beholder in response to things which he and the artist agree to be fundamental data of life. The artist is an artist because he can arouse so much response in so economical a way.

This—again we are recapitulating—is exactly what the church is doing. It is a fact of history that when the Reformed churches were genuine centers of corporate response to life—centers of social conviction and of faith which was related to common life—their preachers were artists, and were acknowledged (even if not in these precise terms) to be so. People expected them to be prophets who gathered up common convictions and gave them eloquent expression. Some were ham actors, some overhistrionic; a closer criticism of some of their activities would have delivered them from excesses which they shared with all other kinds of artist. But the old-fashioned preacher and his congregation were in some sense a corporate body making a corporate response—they were this at their best, and it was only when they fell away from that ideal that they became passive audiences listening to lectures. The preachers of yesterday were, like the prophets of Israel, folk artists. Forty or fifty years ago (in Britain anyhow) somebody broke their nerve, and their activity is now discredited almost universally (again, in Britain).

The Recovery of Worship

So the secret of the recovery of worship in the Reformed churches is not at present in any attempt to revive the pattern of the Reformed worship of 1900. In any case it was too defective a pattern to stand revival. The secret is the recovery of the notion of the *gathered congregation* as prophet or folk artist. In other words, "would that all the Lord's people were prophets"; would that corporately they could recapture the skill, wisdom, discernment, and gift for communication that the prophets of Israel had.

The Disabilities of the Artist Are Largely Illusory

In going about among people who are interested in music-making in church, I hear complaints of all kinds of religious disability. Take two or three familiar examples. The musician is prevented by his lack of resources from performing the music he wishes to perform (especially in Britain); the musician is prevented by what he takes to be public opinion; the organist or the minister asks in despair how he is to get his congregation to learn new hymns; the thoughtful musician wonders how the psalms can be performed in modern public worship. Every one of these difficulties is present only because we have lost our sense of corporate drama; and every one of them can be solved to some extent by glancing at what the theater is doing.

In the matter of learning new congregational music we encounter various problems and various attempts at solution. In Britain the business is largely abandoned; the few who try to interest their congregations in enlarging their repertory of hymns are regarded as eccentrics. By contrast in the United States there are vast pedagogic projects, ac-

companied by long-playing discs and piles of literature, designed to familiarize the laity with the contents of new
hymnals. (Examples are the promotion projects associated
with the Lutheran *Service Book and Hymnal*, and *The
Methodist Hymnal*, 1966.) I would rather have the project
than its absence; but the assumption still is that learning
and experiment cannot be associated directly with worship.

Well then, consider Benjamin Britten's "Let's Make an
Opera," in which a performance of the miniature opera,
"The Little Sweep," is preceded by a rehearsal involving the
audience in learning three cheerful songs which, at the appropriate points in the opera, they join in singing. The rehearsal is not held on some other day, at some other time,
or after the opera is presented. It is part of the whole
presentation. Not so a congregational practice. The practice is occasionally held after evening service, or on some
other day, not at service time; or perhaps before the service
begins. It is never (or am I wrong?) part of the worship
itself. But why can it not be? Practicing may be "irreverent"
or "not devotional"; but we simply have to ask whether
church musicians are going to continue to insist on avoiding everything that disturbs habitual devotions, or whether
they are willing to move on from "Tell me the old, old
story."

Again, if worship is a communal response to things agreed
to be fundamental to life, the organist who simply sees his
duty as giving people good music is beating his brains out
against a brick wall. He wants to get people to like good
music. But why should they? It is all very well if they are
all middle western surburbans or all Englishmen or all Scots
—but suppose some of them are Jamaicans or Puerto
Ricans. Pushing music at people is not the church's work;
but using music as part of a corporate response is very much
its work. People who have not attempted it can still be

astonished at the amount of enterprise you can get out of
a congregation if you will only write the music into the
script. If it can be seen, and doesn't have to be laboriously
shown, to be part of a process of communal response, people begin to show interest, even when they hardly know
why they are doing so. And as for the writing of hymns into
a script, Noye's Fludde has already shown us how this can
be done. The Passions of J. S. Bach show the same thing.
We can now look at all this in detail before coming to our
final conclusion.

Old Music—New Drama

Two questions remain to be dealt with, of which the first
is: How can a new approach to the drama of public worship help us to make new use of familiar music?

What we said about Noye's Fludde in the last chapter
gave a pointer toward the conclusion we are aiming at. We
can now make a few suggestions about hymns, psalms,
anthems, and organ music, all within the familiar tradition,
before adding some about the new kinds of music that are
waiting to be used. Let us take as our starting point the assumption that any service of worship is a drama whose
"script" has at least some recognizable connection with the
pilgrimage of mankind—and the corresponding pilgrimage
of the individual—from the Old Testament to the New.
From the beginnings of Christian worship the real "drive"
of the drama has come from the superposition of the gospel
on the Old Testament. In the primitive church the Bible
was the Old Testament; the common conversation and
remembrance of Christians was the New Testament. In
developed worship the reading of both testaments is a working out of the drama—"You hath he quickened, who were
dead in trespasses" (Eph. 2:1 KJV). Human life untouched
by Christ, even if it be religious, is "Old Testament" still.

Every full service of worship rises out of the human situation and dramatically applies the gospel to it. This is the dramatic intent of the "confession of sins" with which such services normally open. To read the scriptures of the Old Testament and then those of the New is dramatically, or symbolically, to juxtapose and bring into relevant relation the two dispensations of "B.C." and "A.D."—of life to which Christ is about to speak and of life to which he has spoken. In the end we come to the table of Christ to act and be acted upon in the true "theater of faith."

1. Hymns

When we talk of hymns in this context we at once find ourselves in controversy with some of the most formidable minds in the business. For it has been fairly often said by those who would improve our worship and our theology that many hymns are "sub-Christian," and, though popular, unsuitable for use in public worship. One of the most influential writers on this subject, the late Bernard Manning, who most certainly did arouse us from a longstanding apathy and undiscriminating muddle in our attitude toward hymns, was fond of disparaging most hymns that did not come up to the Christian standards exemplified by Charles Wesley. "The greatest hymns," he wrote once, "are Christian, thoroughly and irrevocably Christian; and when I say Christian, I mean that they concern Christ." [2] That is indisputable; but the question unanswered here is whether a service of Christian worship is the better for having its congregational utterances limited to the hymns which are in this sense the greatest. Manning in another place wrote disapprovingly of "O worship the King" and of "Through

[2] *The Hymns of Wesley and Watts* (Naperville, Ill.: Alec R. Allenson, 1960), p. 142. The actual date of writing was 1924.

the night of doubt and sorrow," as being hymns well below the required standard.

But for all my reverence for the memory of this great man
and for the work he did—as timely as it proved to be
historic—I would ask whether we achieve our aim in worship if we insist on the puritan doctrine that all worship
is, so to put it, statically "New Testament" worship. If all
the hymns (and all else) are of the loftiest Christian standard, then our presupposition is that the worshiper steps
into the New Testament as soon as he puts a foot over the
threshold of the church door. This is precisely the in-group,
"family prayers" doctrine of worship. In the world as we
have it, with congregations as we find them, this simply does
not correspond with the facts of life. The world must be
brought into the New Testament through the drama of
worship itself. Those who have a tradition of "common
prayer" have always held this. Reverting for a moment to
Anglican morning and evening prayer, the worshiper in
these is not thrown straight into the New Testament, but is
prepared for it by way of the Old Testament. (To precede
these services with a New Testament hymn is one more way
of upsetting their dramatic rhythm.)

A "dramatic" view of hymns will lead to a new kind of
assessment. It will be possible to approve, and use, hymns
which exhibit the "Old Testament" virtues whether or not
they deal explicitly with "New Testament" subjects. Now
literary grace, effectiveness of expression, memorability of
phrase, and all such virtues are "Old Testament" virtues.
They are what one would expect of any decent secular
poetry. Therefore we require them, in any case, of all
hymns, just as in the Christian ethic there is no question
but that the disciple is required to go the *first* mile. Therefore the hymn, "O God of earth and altar," which is strictly
"Old Testament" but is magnificent literature, is a most

welcome sight in any hymnbook for its piercing relevance
and its unexampled trenchancy of expression. So is "O worship the King," and so are all the great hymns founded on
psalms. Hymns like "City of God," which have suffered
from the frowns of the orthodox, have a new chance of ap-
proval. Such hymns cannot express the conclusion of the
drama, perhaps, but they can express a legitimate stage in
its progress.

On the other hand, hymns which are "New Testament"
in subject matter but fail of the elementary "Old Testament" virtues are quite useless if one is thinking dramatically. The error (if I may presume to refer to it) of
those who would rather sing a second-rate gospel song than
a fine piece like "When wilt thou save the people?" because
the gospel song is about Christ and the other is not, is that
of trying to go the second mile without ever having gone
the first. The Christian ethic does not despise justice,
though it seeks to add generosity. In literature, the Christian approach should not neglect the secular standards although it must always seek, in its use of hymns, to add the
dimension of the New Testament at some point. Indeed,
I think it is a requirement of any Protestant service of the
ordinary kind, in which hymns are so important, that at
least one of them shall be indeed specifically Christian, "irrevocably Christian," in Manning's phrase.

But there is more to be suggested yet. It should not be
taken as self-evident (I have already said) that an unaltera-
ble order of service should be the rule in Protestant
churches. One of the things that one discovers when one
seeks to rewrite the script without changing the subject is
that many hymns almost unusable in the familiar order
become relevant and penetrating in the context of a new
one.

Again, it is, in any hymnbook, only some hymns that any

given congregation can sing easily. There will be a few
that go to tunes the congregation does not know, and some
that go to tunes which that congregation will never enjoy.
What needs to be done by hymns that everybody knows can
be done only by them; it cannot be done by hymns which
most people do not know. But something else can be done
by these. No choir ought to be too proud to be prepared to
sing a hymn to the congregation. I do not here mean that
they should sing one of these multitudinous hymn-anthems
which seem to form an increasing part of the choir's
repertory (see below), but that the choir should sing a
hymn "straight," with only the most modest "production
effects," while the congregation follows its words. As part
of the "drama" this is at least as useful as the congregational singing of a hymn, though in a different way; and it
is certainly far better than the attempted congregational
singing of a hymn that in fact does not get sung at all because it is unknown.

The proper use of hymns demands the kind of approach
to them that Britten shows in *Noye's Fludde*. After what
we said earlier about that, nothing need be added here.[3]

2. Psalms

Part of what has just been said will become clearer if we
turn to the Psalter. Now I understand that in many parts
of the United States, as in many parts of English Dissent,
there is a marked resistance to the use of psalms in Christian worship. I must plead with those who thus set their
faces against the Psalter. Nothing could so effectively de-
humanize and damage Christian worship as the neglect of

[3] I have written more about this in *Hymns Today and Tomorrow*. Perhaps I may repeat my conviction that the universal American practice of
interlining words, by making the words impossible to read as a poem,
frustrates any effective dramatic use of them.

the Psalter. It owes much of its present ineffectiveness in
Protestant circles to the progress which this neglect has already succeeded in achieving.

Basically the error is once again that of trying to go the
second mile without going the first. The psalms, we say,
aren't Christian. The answer is—in that sense—neither is
anybody by nature. Many worshipers are happy enough to
use those psalms which sound most like Christian (or, in
Manning's sense, nearly Christian) hymns. Some of them
capture Christian affections because they are beautiful or
dramatic or edifying. But the great majority of the psalms
are unknown to any worshiper except the very faithful
Anglican who can attend daily morning and evening prayer.

If the rule is that nothing that is not specifically Christian may be sung in church, the psalms have no place.
Let us be quite clear about that. Psalm 23 has no place
there, nor has psalm 103. Nothing is gained by admitting
some psalms because they are beautiful. Who made the
twenty-third psalm beautiful? Not its author, whose language would baffle any English-speaking singer. They are
beautiful because of the assiduity of the old translators
(especially those of the English prayer book version). They
are sometimes more beautiful than intelligible. But they are
beautiful mostly because we are used to them. That is not a
reason for introducing them to worship, if we really believe
that from start to finish, worship must remain on the loftiest
New Testament plane. As it is, in some of our favorite
psalms we have to sing words which would hardly pass the
test of a modern editorial committee. What about the
"enemies" in psalm 23 itself? Are they, as C. S. Lewis once
said, an intrusion? What we normally do is let them slip
through without examination. What good does it do a New
Testament Christian to be told in psalm 103 that "The
Lord . . . made known his ways to Moses, his acts to the

people of Israel"? What does the New Testament Christian understand by "The sun shall not smite thee by day, nor the moon by night"? How about "Surely thou wilt slay the wicked" in psalm 139 (KJV), or the bulls on the altar in psalm 51? (We leave them out, of course. Offensive stuff!)

We leave them out; and we write endlessly protesting against their absurdity. For example, the weighty and influential pen of Leslie Weatherhead has recently gone into action against the "absurdities" of using the psalms, and many familiar hymns, in Christian worship.[4] His argument, which cites psalm 101, psalm 68, and of course psalm 137, and which includes even the *Benedicite* in its condemnations, is a classic example of what I presume here to call the "first mile" error. He appears to believe—as do all the others who write about these things in support of modern apologetic, that when people sing these things in church they are meant to be expressing their personal belief. I suspect that there is a weakness here in the arguments about worship that we hear from the Bishop of Woolwich. But reading or singing the psalms is on the same level as reading an extract from the newspaper in church—and I would argue that in its proper dramatic place neither is inappropriate. It is because I have heard this argument so frequently from intelligent and distinguished members of the American churches, as well as from many Anglicans in England, that I make a point of it here.

Considered as dramatic material, the psalms expose the very heart of the Old Testament, and therefore of human life. As folk songs for a Christian congregation, to be sung heartily, they are scarcely of any use at all. They are best understood by people who are prepared to take the trouble to become familiar with the rest of the Bible—so that refer-

[4] *The Christian Agnostic* (Nashville: Abingdon Press, 1965), esp. pp. 166-67.

ences to the Exodus, the circumstances of the Babylonian
Exile, and at least the outward generalities of Israel's history
are not altogether hidden from them. As a matter of fact, a
skillfully edited psalter in a conservatively revised translation could provide all that is needed in a twelve-page introduction supplemented by brief headings and notes to the
individual psalms. A reasonably sensitive eye—the kind of
eye that nobody shrinks from applying to any library book
—will detect important and enlightening references to the
psalms in the New Testament. A very intractable obstacle
to the understanding and use of the psalms is that obstinate
refusal of contemporary Christians to read the Bible outside
church.

But given this minimum of background information, the
possibilities for the dramatic use of the psalms are endless.
We have already referred to the ancient use of parts of the
psalms as "anthems" in the Eucharist. But many psalms
which were never intended in any case to be sung congregationally can be sung as "anthems" in the modern sense—
carefully interpreted by a good choir to Anglican chants, or
to plainsong, or to Gélineau's psalmody—and their illustrative power is beyond measure. For they speak of human experience, and often of personal experience, and they are
part of the sacred literature upon which the Christian faith
rests; more particularly they are part of the sacred literature
in which our Lord himself was brought up.

Once again it must be urged that if there seem to be
many psalms which fit uneasily into the worship we know,
there is a case for asking what kind of worship they would
fit into, and then trying to devise such a form.

Perhaps it had better also be said that for his purpose
metrical psalms of the Scottish kind are quite useless. They
are (as even Scotsmen are beginning to admit) terrible
literature—they were never meant to be anything but a

literal rendering into meter of the King James Version. And they are so cumbersome that it is practicable to sing only a few verses of any psalm at a time. Only sixteen psalms are ever sung in their entirety in Scottish public worship. All the rest are, in the metrical version, so long as to be unduly wearisome. The metrical version was designed to make folk songs of the psalms, and it did this—it enabled them to be sung very easily to easy tunes. But the history of Scotland in the seventeenth century sufficiently indicates that this is not what we now ought to do with the psalms. Scottish Covenanters could sing the minatory psalms and really believe what they sang—they made themselves as much like the Old Testament warriors as they could. The psalms helped them to project themselves back into the Old Testament, and the confining of the worship of ordinary congregations to the Psalter had the notorious effect of over-emphasizing the Old Testament ethos, and of gravely damaging Scottish life and religion. The effect of this (the ban on anything but psalms and a few New Testament paraphrases was only lifted in the mid-nineteenth century) is only now becoming apparent. It is a very serious matter to confine public praise to the Old Testament.

That sufficiently exposes the other side of the argument. The last thing we should wish for is the projecting of congregations back into the Old Testament. They will not stand for it anyway. They do not wish to be cruel and patriotic and superstitious as were the patriarchs of Israel. But neither should they be encouraged to think that there is nothing in their own lives or in the cultures which surround them that corresponds to the Old Testament. There is, and to deny it is to falsify religion. But once one has admitted that we naturally live in the Old Testament, and have constantly to be recalled, like prodigals, to our Father's house, what one finds is that the Psalter, through 90 percent of its length, has a wisdom, a perceptiveness, and a sense of God's glory which lift us from where we are *toward* the New Testament as nothing else in literature can. The Psalter prepares us to sing our hymns of faith. The hymns that are in this sense like psalms (the ethical, social, national, unitarian ones) perform a similar office.

3. Anthems

If by "anthems" we mean generically the music that is always sung by the choir, our view of the practicalities of worship will cause some dismay, perhaps, to Protestant choirs. It is exceedingly difficult, along the lines we are following, to justify the regular singing of anthems of the usual sort.

But let us examine the difficulty. It comes from the fact that the "production" of the drama that is worship is a matter of ambiguous authority. We have to face the fact that in this "production," which includes the preparation of the sermon, the choosing of the congregational hymns, and the selection of all the rest of the music, there must be one single authority at work. This does not mean that it must all be in one pair of hands. But the normal practice is for the minister to take care of most of the service, but for the selection of the anthem to be left to the choirmaster. If this is done without consultation, or, as it sometimes is, without any agreement even on such principles as the observance of the church's year, what happens is that the anthem (or anthems) becomes simply a break for entertainment through music. To call it "worship through music" is to bandy words. Whatever went on before stops, and the anthem begins without reference to it.

This, to be candid, is pernicious. It reduces the "drama" to a revue or pantomime in which short bursts of dramatic activity follow one another without relevance to each other beyond the needs of astute program building. In Anglican evensong the anthem is agreed to be an addition to the service: "Here followeth the anthem." But where in Protestant worship it comes in the middle of the service, it really is impossible to see it as anything but a performance by the choir. And this is pernicious because it encourages the congregation to listen to a service as passively as it would listen to a revue—to let things happen without making any effort to respond to them. This, in fact, is the cult of "music loving," and it is so firmly in line with the emphasis in music which it is the whole purpose of our argument to alter that we must challenge our church musicians to think again about it.

The way I venture to approach it is this. In respect of the psalms (and in respect of some music we are coming to), we are invited to ask what kind of worship they would fit into, when we find that they do not fit into the worship we are used to. If it be possible to persuade our choirmasters that indiscriminate anthem singing does not fit into the worship we look for, then may we not ask what kind of worship these anthems are appropriate to? Certainly we may. We need not despair, or lock up the choir cupboard for good.

Anthems at their best are expositions of Scripture through music. If we stick for the moment to the anthems that are familiar—compositions running from, say, two to ten minutes in performance—we find that they can be used in two ways. Either they can be integrated by careful consultation into the fabric of a service, being chosen primarily for their words, not for their music (although by the "second mile" rule we shall insist that they be as good musically as we can make them); or they can be used as expositions of Scripture in themselves—chains of anthems allowing the composers to preach to the congregation. There is much more, actually, to be said for the occasional service at which the choir performs a number of anthems carefully chosen to illuminate Scripture and linked by the necessary devices of worship, than for the performance of sacred cantatas at service time. I confess that if I had a choir that could perform John Ireland's "Greater love hath no man," or S. S. Wesley's "Thou wilt keep him in perfect peace," I should want to devise a service around either, allowing the suggestive juxaposition of scripture texts that we find in the words of these compositions to speak for itself as much as possible. There really is no need for a sermon after "Greater love hath no man." (I would, indeed, encourage the development of this kind of expository anthem by modern composers.)

There are no practical difficulties here that are beyond solution. A good choir ought to have a repertory on which it is able to draw at one choir practice's notice for the anthem which will be right for the coming Sunday's service. A minister who knows his trade should be able to adjust things so that the anthem provides a smooth-running vehicle for its part of the dramatic movement. The minister may be tone-deaf, but he can still cooperate with his choir director in this way. The position of the anthem in the service ought to be entirely adjustable, according to its own character and to its part in the drama relative to the other parts. If there is any difficulty with the choir that stands on its dignity and wishes to dictate what kind of music can be sung, the choir can be asked to go and sing somewhere else. Professionalism in choirs should be confined to the maintaining of excellent standards in singing, and not allowed to degenerate into a demand for the congregation's admiration.

But what is more, this principle can really be applied even when the choir is not a strong professional body. Anthems

do not have to be elegant four-part compositions. They can
be carols. They can (we said just now) be hymns or psalms.
The golden rule is only this: that the anthem, or what we
use for an anthem, shall be a contribution to good drama,
shall keep the congregation's mind on the "plot," and shall
be something which is better sung *to* the congregation than
by it.

There has been a good deal of controversy in the history
of church music between those who believed in the primacy
of music and those who thought that in church what was
sung by a choir should make its words clearly audible to the
people. John Wyclif remarked in the fourteenth century,
"When there are forty or fifty in a choir, three or four
proud and lecherous rascals perform the most devout
service with flourishes so that no one can hear the words,
and all the others are dumb and watch them like fools";
and John Wesley in his day expressed a strong distaste for
anthems in which the elaboration of vocal parts obscured
the words. He was especially fond of Handel because in his
works there is so much broad homophonic music, and where
it becomes fugal, the words are always clearly enunciated
in the fugue subject. It is far otherwise with polyphonic
music; and of course today there are many who argue that
the singing of anthems in Latin is out of place in churches
where Latin is otherwise unknown.

One should hesitate to be philistine in such matters; but
in these literate days it does seem right that the congregation should be provided with a copy of the words of
anthems that the choir sings, unless these are strictly
liturgical pieces set to words that the congregation both
knows and, at that point in the service, expects. In any
building of any size it is unwise to rely on the choir to
make every word audible; and in music of any elaboration,
where different voices are singing different parts of the

same verbal phrase, it hardly helps if they do. Yet we must fully concede to the musician to write as he is moved to write, and it is quite unnecessary nowadays to exclude from public worship anthems whose words do not wholly come through in the singing. A copy for the congregation, with a translation where a foreign tongue is used, is all that is needed—but it is needed, and even if it is only something run off on the church's duplicator, it should be somebody's business to see that this is done. In English Dissenting churches it was the custom until a generation ago to provide a repertory of anthems in the hymnbook, and the words of the anthems in the words-only copies. The available repertory is now so large that this custom has been dropped; but it is undesirable to encourage the substitution of music loving for liturgy by leaving the congregation ignorant of all but the opening words of any choir piece.

4. Incidental Music

The only thing that need be said about organ music (or music played on any other instrument in a church service) is that it should never be regarded as absolutely necessary, and unless it is clearly and demonstrably better than silence, it is bettter omitted. It needs to be chosen and played with a view to its place in the people's worship. And since it is not associated with words in the ordinary way, and the congregation has gathered to take part in the drama of worship but not primarily to listen instructedly to music, the performer must be content not to be listened to, and not even to attract attention as he is entitled to do in a recital.

Church music's task is to reinforce either the words or the action of the drama. In Protestant worship, anyhow, the words necessarily come first. It is hardly inappropriate to say that they come first in Catholic worship as well; but it has to be pointed out that Protestants of the literate kind commit the greater inconsistency when they approach church music sentimentally.

Organ music well and discreetly played is not only very pleasant to the ear. To Protestants it acts as a very real help in finding their way from the world's level to that level to which worship is designed to bring them, especially when it is the first thing they hear as they come into church. (Dr. Nathaniel Micklem, when he was principal of Mansfield College, once said, memorably, that the introductory organ music does for Protestants what the scent of incense does for Catholics; it lifts them over the threshold of the church.)

But one thing which should always be suspected is the use of music to cover up or obscure some part of worship which is essential but which some think better not noticed. Music of any kind, played or sung, is abused if it is used only for this purpose. It is thoroughly "bad theater" to be doing something to cover something else up. The disagreeable custom of playing organ music during the distribution of the Elements of the Communion at Protestant services is the worst of these abuses. It is a genteel fastidiousness that regards the mechanics of "distribution" as something which it is kinder not to notice. We cannot be altogether happy about the similar use of music to cover up the presentation of the people's offerings or church dues. This act needs to be carefully built into the "drama"; too often it is an intrusion about which everybody is somewhat embarrassed. This is not the place to enter on a discussion of the proper theology of money, but clearly it is "bad theater" to do something which is necessary and at the same time be sufficiently ashamed of it to want your mind distracted by music during its performance.

To sing "Agnus Dei" during the Communion, as Catholics do, is something quite different. Here words are dropped into the communicant's consciousness which are (or are deemed to be in those circles) exactly appropriate to his thoughts. They suggest sacrifice and redemption, and that is exactly the point to which in the Mass or the Eucharist he has been brought. It is not impossible that in Protestant worship suitable offertory sentences should be sung at the taking of the collection, or (if, as will probably come about eventually, the collection is only *presented*, not actually *collected* during the service) at its formal presentation.

It is far better than this to make use of instrumental music in a clearly liturgical way: to use it as a signal, or to call attention to a particular point. I can imagine, for example, the magnificently dramatic use of psalm 24:7-10 in Scotland at the bringing-in of the Elements, preceded, on some high day, by a fanfare of trumpets or something similar on the organ. Certain kinds of impressionistic contemporary organ music can assist the worshiper in keeping reflective silence for a short period at some appropriate point in the service. This is the proper "dramatic" use of music; the playing of "voluntaries" to cover up unseemly liturgical necessities is not.

It is useful to recall the use made in Continental circles of incidental music, especially in the matter of the Chorale Prelude. The Chorale Prelude (of which Bach's are the most famous, but not the only examples) is strictly an introduction to the singing of a hymn; it is only derivatively (as in Bach's larger examples) a separate, freestanding meditation on the hymn. The chorale prelude we mentioned illustratively back in chapter 3 is one of this kind—a decorative introduction to a normal hymn. There are very great dramatic possibilities here for experiment in contemporary worship. The "intonations" prescribed for use in the Swiss Reformed Church in *Intonationen zu den Melodien im Gesangbuch der evangelisch-reformierten Kirchen der deutschen Schweiz* (1955) give a hint of what can be done. The prosaic and often quite unnecessary four-part recitation of the whole of a hymn tune by the organist before the congregation sings can be replaced by instrumental utterances which serve the drama of worship much better. Few organists, even in our countries where we do not have the advantage that Germans have of always knowing exactly what tune is to be sung to a hymn, realize that it is never necessary to play as an introduction even part of the score exactly as it is written for the voices. I would here quote just one example recently heard, of a quite unforgettable touch of drama in an organist's introduction to a very well-known hymn. The service was being held at Glasgow University, and the organist, Frederick Rimmer (a musician whose talent for drama was illustrated in the third anthem quoted at the beginning of this book), introduced it as follows:

Fig. 21

That was enough to make an old hymn sound resoundingly new.

The point to be made about instrumental music in church, then, is this: that opportunities for serving the drama are always to be taken, and opportunities for holding up the drama for the sake of music should be neglected. Public worship is not a musical after all.

11. new music

The Church in Secular Society

After these investigations we are left, as I hope, with some equipment to answer the most fundamental question of all, which is: how far is church music necessary to the well-being of the contemporary church?

The fact that the great majority of Christians have for two thousand years assumed it to be necessary, and that the majority of these have on balance put it to good use, does not dispense us from the need to repeat the question. It has to be answered in full recognition of the secularization of society which is one of the great new facts of our time.

A historical view of music making in the culture which we here share with Europe insists that music is, just as much as hospitals, social services, science, and literacy, a subject of secularization. Those other things were at one time the concern of the professionally Christian; they became the concern of the aristocratically benevolent (or the aristocratically learned), and after that, the concern of the wealthy benevolent or the wealthy learned; and now their administration and their benefits are both in the hands of those who need claim neither a religious affiliation nor any social standing, and who need not be personally able to afford to pay for them. It is exactly so with music.

Medieval music was, though not wholly directed and made by churchmen, always judged by reference to the surrounding churchly establishment (or climate of faith). Classical music was made and heard at the bidding of an aristocratic patron (who might have been a churchman). Romantic music was there for whoever could pay for it. Music in our time is a field in some part of which everybody moves. The most important discovery about music nowadays is the way in which it can be used, or misused, by people who have no disciplinary background, such as an assumed religion, the responsibilities of social status, or the standards appropriate to wealth gave to the music purveyors of former times.

What we say about church music today must depend, then, on what we say the church is here to do in the world. Bishop Newbigin is among the first and most celebrated of those who are constantly urging us not to be dismayed by the church's loss of prestige. If the secular world has learned the value of hospitals and social services and culture from the church, it was precisely the church's duty to teach it these things. It is now the church's business to treat the secular world as an adult pupil and not to try to keep it *in statu pupillari*. The church's mission to the world has become progressively less a mission of teaching in such spheres as those, and in that of music; but what kind of new mission is the church continuing to exercise? The church is still behaving a little like a retired schoolteacher: uneasy in any situation in which it is not his main business to lay down the law; impatient of contradiction and debate; inept at conversation on equal terms.[1]

[1] See Lesslie Newbigin, A *Faith for This One World?* (New York: Harper & Row, 1961); Harvey Cox, *The Secular City* (New York: The Macmillan Company, 1965); and Colin Williams, *Faith in a Secular Age* (Harper & Row, 1966).

About this ineptitude the church has a very bad
conscience at present. We know, dogmatically, that the
church has a mission which is very different from that of
teaching people what they will one day learn fully and not
need to be taught any more. But we—and I am afraid this
is especially true of Protestants—have become so deeply
attached to our pedagogic and patronizing habits that we
have had to discover how painful it is going to be to alter
these habits. Aristotle said that all learning is painful; but
few subjects are more painful than that which the arthritic
pedagogue must learn if he is to climb down from his desk.
We are about to find that, having concentrated so firmly
on teaching the world what we assume it does not know,
we have a very long leeway to make up in learning the
technique which really was always our true ministry: con-
versing with the world.

It is no longer necessary to teach the world to be benevolent, to teach it to value education, to teach it to care for
the sick and the insane, or to teach it to enjoy music. The
lessons have been learned. But there is no way by which
the teacher, qua teacher, even if it be the Church of Christ,
can ensure that the pupil will maintain the truth in a
stable equilibrium. You can teach a child what is right
and what is wrong, but that of itself does not prevent his
falling into error. Christian legislators can conceive Christian cities and Christian cultures, but they cannot, merely
as legislators, ensure that there will be no slums and no
drug addicts in the cities they plan.

We Protestants have always been teachers and lawgivers.
Our worship has always been obsessively sermon centered.
We cannot hold a fifteen-minute campus service without
expecting its leader to instruct us in some way. The consequence of pedagogic overemphasis is an oppressive sense
of anxiety during periods when pupils seem to be unusually

refractory, and ours is evidently such a time as that. Here
has the church been preaching Christianity for all these
centuries, we say, and what have we to show for it? Anarchic
affluence, addictive acquisitiveness, and all the rest of the
vocabulary of the querulous moralist. We rumble on, not
heeding the warning that we ought to have heeded: that
for the church to go on approaching the world in the
spirit of a learned teacher approaching an ignorant pupil
is to misinterpret the whole ministry of the church. The
King James Version, misinterpreted by fundamentalists,
has much to ask for. When we are told that Jesus said,
"Go and teach all nations," we find no difficulty in seeing
ourselves as a chosen race of schoolmasters.[2]

Farewell to Pedagogy

It was for this reason that I spent so much time in this
book emphasizing the element of drama—which could
also be called the existential element—in worship. I make
no judgments about what attitudes or approaches were appropriate in past ages, or will be appropriate in future
ages; but I am quite clear that for our present age, the
age of Will rather than of Emotion or Knowledge, neither
the romantic approach nor the pedagogic one will meet
the need. The romantic approach takes too little account
of failure; the pedagogic approach is too impatient of ig-
norance and disobedience. Habits in church behavior which
assume the superior insight or knowledge, or even the
superior moral tone, of the ingroup will engender a speech
which communicates nothing to our present age. The
church cannot bridge the gulf between itself and "the
rest" with a built-in authority. The church must learn to

[2] See, if you will, the central argument in my book, *Into a Far Country*
(London: The Independent Press, 1962), some of whose conclusions I
am here treating as stated.

do without its anxiety that what it says may be neglected or misunderstood. It must manage without the security of sacerdotalism and mystique.

Since I do not believe that our Lord's own method of communicating was primarily, or even to any noticeable extent at all, pedagogic, I do not think that this ought to shock anybody in the church. We may have our pedagogic phases—yes, there is an order of "teachers" in the church according to Paul in I Corinthians 12, and there is a time and place for the church to act as teacher. But the real communication between the church and the world is what can only be described by the electrical analogy of "induction." What our Lord did in his ministry was to juxtapose goodness against the world's evil, and by this means "induce" grace in the world. It was his ministry, primarily, to be God Incarnate, and thereby to show what the true Messiah, the real deliverer of the world, must be. He placed life alongside deadness, and thereby induced life in the dead thing. He did not accomplish this deliverance (from sin, we say—from the settled condition of grievance against God and all his works) by teaching us what we did not know. He did it by being God Incarnate in the world, and letting the consequences follow. This was what Hebrews calls "obedience" (Heb. 5:8). What we call the "teaching" of Christ consisted entirely of either illustrations in parables and actions of the principles upon which God makes his love known to the world, or of traditional reminiscences, and reconstructions, faithfully communicated by the evangelists, of things which during his earthly life he said and did. Provided that we do not insist on regarding him first and last as a teacher of righteousness (or of anything else), we need not be disconcerted by the problems surrounding the quest of the historical Jesus. As John says, "He was in the world." That is the heart of it. We may doubt the details of many of the records but this we do not doubt. Nobody doubts it. Some have doubted even whether he died or whether he died when Christians believe he did; but the one thing nobody doubts is that he was in the world. The consequence of his being in the world can be expressed only as John expresses it: the world refused to know him, but it could not extinguish the light.

Very well; the church is primarily concerned with being in the world—with *being* in the sense that we associate with Tillich: being positively, being actively, being itself.

The visible church is the community in which men practice the gospel. It is, as it were, somewhere between Jeremiah 31 and Revelation 21. Jeremiah (31:31-4) speaks of a time when men shall no longer teach one another, but shall know the Lord for themselves; the vision in Revelation is of a city in which there is not even a temple. Between these two frontiers stands the church which, in the ages between the first full revelation and the final consummation, is required to be the kingdom in the world in the same sense in which (to use Amos Wilder's fine phrase) Jesus Christ was the kingdom in his own person while he was on earth. It is then less important that the church shall show the marks of an efficient worldly legislator or teacher ("my kingdom is not of this world") than that it shall show forth the marks of the incarnation of God in Christ, shall "bear in its body the marks of the dying of the Lord Jesus." That is where we find room for the conception that the church may be subject in its course to momentary transfigurations as well as to the cross; we find all the room in the world for the idea that the church is the bodying forth of the principle of love—a body of love which the world may refuse to know but whose light cannot be extinguished.

The efficient teacher or legislator, especially on the scale
of "all the kingdoms of the world" makes friends and influences people—but that is not the church's ministry. He
looks for status, but the church does not. He measures
successes, but the church does not. He acts by direction;
the church acts by "induction."

Let Music Be Music

What effect do thoughts like this have on the question
of whether church music is necessary? The most obvious
effect they have is to show us that church music misleads
believers and unbelievers alike if it is mixed up with status
symbols, influencing people and pedagogy. If it is there
merely to provide pleasure for music-lovers it will miss the
point it is designed to meet.

Most of the categories within which we have talked of
good and bad church music in the past have outlived
what usefulness they had. Usually they are not biblical or
in any sense primary, but merely functions of expedience.
To take a crude example, to talk of classical music as good
and jazz as bad is not to make a judgment which can be
fitted at any point into the necessities of Christian worship.
To the statement, "Classical music is good and jazz is
bad," the only answer is, "Who says so?"

The great thing about contemporary music is, as we
began by saying, that it really does ask radical questions,
and drives us back well behind the complacent categories
in which we have been content to judge church music.
The one judgment that we need to make about church
music is that it is good if it really is music. Let music be
in the world in the same sense that the church is and that
Christ is in the world. Music is subject to only one moral
law—it is required to be. Defect in music, as in the church,
is simply what Thomas Aquinas called *privatio boni*—the

absence of good where good ought to be. You can distinguish a good hymn tune much more easily than you can distinguish a bad one. (The heart of the Christian ethic is in that it identifies goodness where all other ethics are content to identify, and punish, badness.) You know that "Praise, my soul" and "Onward, Christian soldiers" and "Dundee (French)" and "Wachet Auf" are good hymn tunes; it hardly needs proving until some pedagogue comes along and says that "Onward, Christian soldiers" is a bad hymn tune because he has applied to it some esoteric rule that only classical musicians know about. One can only at best be fairly sure that some hymn tunes are bad—and their badness is in having missed opportunities, having substituted rhetoric for reason, having buried a talent instead of fructifying it. Bad music is music that to some extent fails to *be*—it has a touch of infantilism or imbecility. It is a thankless task identifying its badness; what matters, and what is worth spending time on, is enjoying and celebrating and publicizing music that really is music, whatever form it takes. It is very probable that forms of music which make churchmen uneasy at present will themselves prove more profitable if the church itself can get rid of its anxieties. The worst affliction of church music at present is the idea that still lurks in the background that there is a distinctive "church style." It has made many composers unable to give their best work to the church (although Sir Thomas Beecham's dictum that no composer ever gave his best to the church is a wild and ludicrous generalization). But a church that is content to *be*, and not to dictate, will encourage musicians to *be*. There are plenty of signs that this is already happening, and that the church is less wedded to archaic and hackneyed idioms than it once was. But if the church will only listen more and talk less, it may well find that the asperities and defensive stridencies of some modern forms of music, and of some kinds of modern musicians, will noticeably soften. The assumption that jazz or twelve-tone or electronic or even pop music is hostile to the church's traditions induces a corresponding artificial hostility in the purveyors of this music.

At any rate, if the church sees its worship in terms of drama rather than in terms of instruction, new kinds of music are going to be able to make a contribution which the conventional Protestant outlook prevented them from making.

"The Treason of the Clerks"

But before giving examples of what that means, I wish to digress for a moment in order to air a grievance that has lately begun to haunt me. I have said nothing in all these pages about poetry—nor, come to that, about religious drama properly so called—and this is because I am sufficiently aware of my own limitations to leave this to others. But it is time, I think, to ask whether the composers of our contemporary church works are not leaving a duty undone in being so unwilling to take hold of contemporary poetry for their libretti.

An example comes to mind. In the spring of 1965, a group of schoolboys and girls I knew of let it be known that they had prepared Kenneth Leighton's very beautiful cantata, *Crucifixus pro Nobis* [3] for performance. I invited them to sing it on the morning of Palm Sunday in church. It is a most winning piece of music, far from easy to sing, and the performance made a considerable impression on a congregation which is not accustomed to hearing music at

[3] Kenneth Leighton is Lecturer in Music at Edinburgh University. This is his Op. 18, composed in 1960. He is established as one of the leading composers in English church music. See *Twentieth Century Church Music*, pp. 75, 226.

that level in church. It was necessary so to devise the order of morning service as to provide a setting for this work. The first necessity in such a case is to find hymns whose music will not contrast too conspicuously with the quality of the special music. Passiontide provides few problems there— there are some really great tunes, known to everybody, which are expected at that season. It was not the music, but the words, which provided the problem. For here was a first-class contemporary composer writing his best music for four seventeenth-century poems all of which dwelt lovingly and obsessively on the sufferings of the Crucified, inviting us to show pity to him. The words were better literature than the notorious libretto of Stainer's *Crucifixion* (the nonbiblical parts of which provide a strong candidacy for the honor of being the worst poetry in the English tongue), but there is nothing to choose between them when it comes to theology. This lovely music was carrying words which say exactly what the Scriptures and doctrine of the church tell us not to say about the Passion.

> What bruises do I see!
> What hideous stripes are those!
> Could any cruel be
> Enough, to give such blows?

Good poetry can be bad doctrine (of course this is bad doctrine! See Luke 23:27-31)—but while there may be a place in the church's drama for contemporary poetry that illustrates life's defects, it really is difficult to justify the enshrining of venerable but doctrinally unhealthy poetry of this kind in a musical work that is composed in the most serious and exalted style. The only thing to do in practice, when it was part of a service of worship, was to allow it to speak, and then attempt, without in any way laboring the point, to set forth the rest of the Gospel in the rest of the service. Therefore the service began with the hymn, "Sing, my tongue, how glorious battle glorious victory became" and ended with the hymn, "The head that once was crowned with thorns is crowned with glory now."

But the problem is a real one. It was the expression of this point of dissatisfaction by a percipient member of the congregation that aroused the thought in my own mind. Our best composers in the classical style are still looking to other ages for their libretti. We get numerous new and excellent settings of the liturgy, but our cantatas and anthems rarely essay an encounter with contemporary poetry. There is a lyric genius in old poetry that evokes the educated musical imagination. And to be sure there is a dogmatic genius as well if you go to the right poets—to John Donne, for example, or George Herbert. But even Benjamin Britten, who has such a keen eye for literature, finds his literary inspirations in the poetry of the past; *Rejoice in the Lamb* is one of the minor miracles of modern church music, and it was a bold gesture to take the poetry of Christopher Smart (an eighteenth-century English minor poet) for its libretto. It is beautiful and seemly, but it speaks the tongue of another age. I ventured to make a guess, in *Twentieth Century Church Music*, about the reason why the same composer took a poet of the First World War, Wilfred Owen, to celebrate the contemporary iniquities of war as they were symbolized in the destruction of Coventry in 1940. It is not a major error to delve into history for words to set to modern music. Indeed, when Parry and Charles Wood set the example at the beginning of this century it was a most refreshing gesture (a gesture of the "age of knowledge"). But is it altogether unfair to suggest that modern musicians of the moderately conservative kind like Leighton, Britten, Berkeley, Joubert, Gardner, and their contemporaries feel that contemporary poetry just won't sing? It is composers of a more avant-garde kind who look to modern literature. There is a real sense of adventure and peril in Vincent Persichetti's remarkable little collection of *Hymns and Responses for the Church Year*,[4] in which we find some startling music, but also words by W. H. Auden and e e cummings. How long do we wait before something in church music corresponds to Elisabeth Lutyens' settings of Wittgenstein's prose in her *Motet*, Op. 27? The possibilities in liturgical drama for contemporary poetry set to music are surely greater than our leading composers appear to assume.

New Styles

The immediate prospects for church music indicate that there is a considerable future for one new style—which is a revival of an old style—namely, the antiphonal psalm or hymn. There is an assumption, again firmly held by Protestants, that the only legitimate form of congregational song is the metrical and continuous hymn. There is no ground at all for this assumption. The form of song in which the congregation alternates with the choir, or with a soloist, is a very ancient form, and it has all manner of practical advantages, not the last of which is that it makes possible a congregational performance music of somewhat greater flexibility and complexity than the ordinary hymn tune.

The best modern example of this is the psalmody of Joseph Gélineau. It has its detractors, among whom I do not count myself. Gélineau's psalmody is already well enough known in Britain and America for people to have seen how it can enrich the drama of worship. The music carries a graceful and moving translation in the original Hebrew meter; the psalms are in verse and chorus form.

[4] (Philadelphia: Elkan-Vogel, 1956.)

Some can be sung with the most barbaric gusto by a congregation; some are better sung by a soloist and the choir in alternation. But one has only to hear a large congregation singing psalm 135 (136, RSV) in Gélineau's version, and then a soloist impersonating the Babylonian exiles in psalm 136 (137, RSV), verses 1-6, to recognize the potentialities of this music: it gives scope for the use of instruments other than, or in addition to, the organ; it is always exceedingly simple; its harmony and melody are contemporary without being harsh, yet traditional without being monkish. The style is capable of imitation, and some successful developments are already to be found.[5] Antiphonal work needs a touch of production to be successful, but this is not a prospect that should at this time of day deter Protestants from trying it.

Jean Langlais' historic canticle, "Dieu, nous avons vu ta gloire," first sung at Strasbourg at the Bible and Liturgy Conference in July, 1957, and now available in an English translation, is another first-rate example of what can be done with antiphonal effects.[6] The use of the "conversational" technique in new music may prove to be a major force in reviving the spirit of drama in liturgy.

When it comes to jazz, we must once again[7] commend the work of Heinz Werner Zimmermann, whose motets and *Psalmkonzert* (a twenty-minute cantata) use certain jazz techniques integrated with a classically contrapuntal style of voice writing. He confesses [8] that he adopts it be-

[5] For example, by Anthony Milner in "O give thanks to the Lord" (Novello, PCB 1413, 1963) and by Christopher Dearnley in the Salisbury Diocesan Festival booklet, 1964.

[6] Referred to in *Twentieth Century Church Music*, pp. 136-37. The original score is published by Editions Philippo, Paris; the English translation is in *Dunblane Praises*, I, 8. Recorded, Editions Studio SM 33.50.

[7] See *Twentieth Century Church Music*, pp. 92-93.

[8] On the jacket note of the record of *Psalmkonzert* (1958)—Cantate 640229

cause it is the only musical style known to him that adequately expresses pure joy. This is worth putting alongside
the statements about jazz recorded earlier (pp. 110 ff). It is
a very good example of how a style thought by so many
to be hostile to church traditions can prove to be not only
adaptable to it, but, in the adaptation, to lose its secular
defects (in this case the tendency to melancholy and
hysteria) and become transfigured without losing its iden-
tity. Zimmermann's music is magnificent church drama in
its own right—full of contrasting color and a sense of
rhythmic crisis which expresses the world's strife but, in
the end, resurrection peace.

Sydney Carter has been showing us similarly how contemporary folk song can be "baptized." Here we have
a different point to make. The tremendous irony of a song
like "Good Friday," with its refrain—

> It's God they ought to crucify
> Instead of You and me,
> I said to the carpenter
> A-hanging on the tree.

—is not congregational song; it is not credal affirmation.
It is a representation of the world's mixed-up predicament.
You stare at Carter's folk songs and wonder how they can
find a place in worship. Then you remember, just in time,
the "second mile" error, and it becomes clear that what
they can do is to illuminate the confession of sins. The confession can be a formal, almost superstitious business. What
you want to say when you come into church is, "Taking it
all round, remembering the police states and the slums and
the hungry people and the race riots and the racketeers, the
waste, the perversion and the iniquity in society we are

miserable sinners, and that is putting it mildly." Public confession is not two hundred people each saying, "I cheated
on my tax return last week"; it is saying, "We are up against
it; we don't know whose fault it is, but we are responsible
—help us!" That kind of thought can be objectified at
once through a protest song, an ironic song, a song of
doubt. Very largely the place of folk song of the sort that
is being put about at the present time is in that part of
the service when the world comes before God as it is and
says, "Lord, have mercy upon us." (This is not the only way
to do it—another way is to get the boys or women in the
choir to sing the heartrending "Kyrie" from Britten's *Missa
Brevis*.)

Even the intractable pop style has made a few authentic
incursions into church music. Leonard Bernstein's *Chiches-
ter Psalms* certainly humanize the Hebrew psalms by setting them to music that has most of the innocence and
sensitiveness of that of *West Side Story*—but the *Chiches-
ter Psalms* require too much production, too much orchestral and choral apparatus to be liturgical. The piece that
most daringly shook the conservative convictions about
pop (which to a large extent I share, as I have said above)
was Ernest Marvin's *A Man Dies*.

A Man Dies—For What?

American readers may need to be told that this is a
dramatic presentation of the gospel designed first for a
teeming youth club on the outskirts of Bristol and later
shown on the BBC television network. Later still it became
a film for church use. The authors are the Reverend Ernest
Marvin (who ran the youth club) and Ewan Hooper. It
runs some twenty-five minutes, and, making very few demands on speakers, achieves its effect chiefly through movement and singing. It is essentially a mine rather than a

play. The figure of Christ, in symbolic poses and movements, is seen over against a large mass of ordinary young
people dancing and jiving to a pop band. Commentary is
provided in the form of a narrative song sung into a micro-
phone by a pop singer. The whole presentation cleverly
shows how the very brutality of the pop style can contribute something positive to Christian drama.[9] It further
shows that not only ballet (which sufficiently shocked the
public when it was included in a service of worship associated with the opening of Coventry Cathedral in 1962)
but also pop dancing can say something in a church setting.

A further point about the history of this remarkable adventure brings us back to our main argument. Everybody
of Christian zeal wanted to know, at the time, what it
had meant to the youngster who was given the part of
Christ in the film. Did it, the TV interviewer asked, make
any difference to him that he had been chosen to do this?
Any who expected to hear him say that it had converted
him were disappointed. The answer was a bewildered and
inarticulate silence.

That is exactly the point we have been making. The
church's business is to be in the world: "rejoice not, that
the spirits are subject unto you; but rather rejoice, because
your names are written in heaven" (Luke 10:20 KJV).
A Man Dies does not preach. It states, and leaves the conclusion to the imagination. It is not designed to be assessed
in terms of converts, of precise numbers of the "saved."
Censuses of the saved are as irrelevant as censuses of Israel
in the days of King David (II Sam. 24). All one is entitled to say is that the harsh young voice, the glazed and
expressionless face of the singer, the hideous overamplified

[9] The libretto of this piece is now published by Darton, Longman and
Todd. See an extended reference to it, with a quotation from one of the
songs, in Twentieth Century Church Music, pp. 187-90.

noise of the guitar, the ugly jerking movements of the
dancers, the dumb miming of the central figure contribute,
in this piece, to authentic drama that Britain as a whole
has found so memorable that still, several years after its
first performance, it is necessary to wait a year before one
can hire the film for church presentation.

"Would That All the Lord's People Were Artists!"

The sum of the matter, for the present, seems to be this:
we are advocating two lines of approach to modern worship. On the one hand we look for a Sunday worship of the
whole Christian community which is far more clearly a
drama of the faith than what we are mostly accustomed to;
that juxtaposes the two kinds of reality, the world as it is
with the world as it is in the mind of God. Worship should
constantly point to the paradox that both are real: that
terror and love are real. It should express the "strange and
dreadful strife." It should constantly make us wonder
which will win, and in the end show us which has won.
It should be more perilous, more alarming, more penitential, and then more wise, serene, and assured than what we
usually rise to. It should be more demanding, more liable
to put people off, and at the same time more comforting,
more rock-like in faith. If it is less defensive, less frightened
of giving the wrong impression, less afraid of controversy,
it will be more truly faithful. Its music, we infer, needs to
be more liable to shock, more an occasion on which anything might happen, and at the same time more rooted and
grounded in the real experience of the people.

We need to give the organist, the choir and the singing
congregation a new view of their task. There is a place for
the songs that the congregation is bound to know—songs
whose repertory varies from place to place—timeless songs
from any century, the great hymns that still hearten us

and bind us together in faith. No church musician should be too high-minded to take infinite pains to see that these do their work effectively. There is a place for the choir to illustrate the drama in music which, however complex its workmanship, is simple enough in impact to make its point. The new music will, I think, combine a new kind of penitence with a new kind of joy and incitement to joy. And the secret key to the transformation of church music is this: that we admit and rejoice in the fact (which has never been untrue) that we are all artists. Remembering that the prophet was the artist of Israel, and that the artist is unquestionably the prophet of our modern times, consider the implication of the memorable phrase attributed to Moses in the Book of Numbers: "Would that all the Lord's people were prophets!"

Traditionally in Protestantism there was one artist in any service of worship: the preacher—and he would have been insulted if you had called him that. But art is not something that a few prophets can rise to. It was that, if you like, in the days of King Saul and of the prophets among whom he was so unexpectedly found. But we are not living in the days when "there was no open vision." Art, being one of the manifestations of the Holy Spirit's work in the world, is a dimension of life—every man is an artist, a self-giver, a self-revealer, if he is allowed to be. In restoring an aesthetic to worship we need no longer mean that we are looking for more beautiful singing and more performances of classical cantatas. We mean, now, that we want men to find that in the church's great public and corporate activity of demonstrating the faith, they can be —wholly, joyfully, astonishingly—themselves.

Faith, said Tillich, is the resultant produced by the three forces of Emotion, Knowledge, and Will. It seemed worthwhile to conduct this argument because we appear to stand at one of those points in the cycles of history where all these forces are running at high pressure, and where, therefore, there is great opportunity for either confusion or creative harmony. We know a great deal, we feel a great deal, and we are passionately concerned for the future—concerned the more because it has never been so doubtful whether we have a future. But if we are to live in all these dimensions, then we must, at any rate while this age lasts, substitute a stereoscopic for a binocular vision of the church's work and its speaking. To proceed from one dogmatic statement of things to the next reactionary dogmatic statement is to manufacture all those speeches and attitudes in the church which make it a mystery at best, a scandal at worst, to the secular world. The church's concern for beauty will never prosper unless the concerns for truth and goodness are kept running—to switch out two while one attends to the other is to live safely, but statically. These are the greatest days for church music since the sixteenth century, and for exactly the same historical reason: the wheel of history has come round again. The danger is part of the adventure.

postscript

The foregoing pages contain material based on lectures given in the United States, and they are being published in the United States; but they are written by an Englishman whose knowledge of the details of musical developments in the U.S.A. is necessarily scanty. I have never been able, nor am I likely ever to be able, to travel at leisure in the U.S.A. My visits there have been, and presumably always will be, on business—made in short periods carved out of time normally devoted to the necessities of busy but impecunious English pastorates. I am therefore very conscious of the limitations of the knowledge that lies behind any statement I make about the American situation.

I suspect that however much personal research I was able to do, the conviction I have that generalizations about the American situation are valueless would not be altered. I believe that at the time when I was writing these lectures the beginnings of a reaction against the staggering and indeed terrifying success mystique of American Protestant churchmanship was beginning to manifest itself. I believe that questions are being answered. I hope so. Merely to make a great deal of music with great efficiency is not necessarily to serve the church's best interests. In Britain we are becoming accustomed now to visits from American choirs who tour the country singing, usually from memory, complicated and sophisticated programs of choral music in our major cities. Always they sing with a prodigious discipline, often with an almost military assiduity. Usually they sing very well—not always; often they produce creative programs indicating a real sensitiveness to the developments of church music—not always. Their high professional polish puts us to shame; their sense of the inwardness of church music is not necessarily equal to their external gloss.

This is the sort of thing that occurs to us in our ancient, decrepit, and struggling country. And, as I have ventured to say in a book called *Music Leadership in the Church*, our own greatest danger is a kind of inverted snobbery that positively exalts our mediocrity and shabbiness into a virtue; that presumes to sneer at the gowns and visual beauty of American choristers from the security of our own diminishing prosperity. That I fully grant. But when all that has been examined and evaluated, I find that when I am in the U.S.A., I spend nine tenths of my time simply gasping with admiration at the sumptuousness of American church music in the great centers to which it has been my privilege to go, and the other tenth asking all sorts of questions.

So when I see these questions coming from American citizens, I feel encouraged. Now one of the most conspicuous examples of success in church music is to be found in The Methodist Church, notably in the quite unexampled effort made in producing *The Methodist Hymnal, 1966*. For sheer size of project, nothing in hymnology has come near it, at any time in history. Not that The Methodist Church is the only denomination to be entering on massive musical projects—even I know that. Both branches of the Lutheran Church—the American Lutheran Church and the Missouri Synod—are expanding their music activities to a dramatic extent. The American Lutheran Church has inaugurated a nationwide hymn-of-the-month project, headed up by Pastor Mandus Egge and his committee, to educate the whole denomination in the use of the Lutheran *Service Book and Hymnal*. The Missouri Synod is currently engaged in educational projects designed (I cannot know with what hope of success) to make everything that is going on now look like chicken feed.

Candidly, this would be terrible if nobody was asking any questions; and therefore it is encouraging to see that now and again the massive Methodist Publishing House produces material that does invite people not merely to accept but also to think. *Music Ministry*, The Methodist Church's monthly journal of church music, is chiefly an educational publication, and in its time it has produced that admirable series, "How Shall We Sing the Lord's Song?" by Charles M. Fisher (Jan.–March, 1964); and in its March, 1966 issue there are two searching articles on the philosophy and functions of the arts in church by Margaret Rigg and J. J. Silber. Both these articles deal with the relation between the artist and common life and the church's concern with that relation. (On the whole I find Margaret Rigg's article sympathetic; and want to ask Mr. Silber a number of questions—but neither should be ignored by any serious student.) These people are asking, "But what is art *doing*?" And however much the ivory-tower kind of artist may be irritated by these questions, when the artist comes in touch with the church (which is a body of ordinary, unspecialized people), he incurs the risk of hearing them, and there is nothing that anybody can do to change that situation.

Music-making in the church will suffocate in its own feather bed if music-makers in a church context are content to be a community of internal congratulation. If you never meet anybody who thinks, and says, that you are talking nonsense you will lose your faculty of self-criticism, and with it your capacity to create. Mortal life is so organized, and, again, there is nothing we can do to change it.

The most inspiriting thing, then, in the American scene is freedom of debate; where there is no sign of it, no amount of exterior gloss will prevent its being depressing. What the music journals of the various churches and the music publishing houses do to keep the scene alive, to invite controversy, to keep debate open, to get radical and, when necessary, awkward questions asked, is well done. I am glad to pay tribute to all those I know who are doing it, and to all those, many more of whom I have not yet learned but whom at some time I hope to meet.

topical index

This is meant to be complementary to the synoptic Contents and is not intended to do more than remind the reader where he can find references to the main contentions of the foregoing essay.